Cat
Daddy

JEREMY P. TARCHER / PENGUIN

a member of Penguin Group (USA) Inc.   New York

Cat

Daddy

What the World's Most
Incorrigible Cat Taught Me About
Life, Love, and Coming Clean

Jackson
Galaxy

with Joel Derfner

JEREMY P. TARCHER/PENGUIN
Published by the Penguin Group
Penguin Group (USA) Inc., 375 Hudson Street, New York, New York
10014, USA · Penguin Group (Canada), 90 Eglinton Avenue East, Suite 700,
Toronto, Ontario M4P 2Y3, Canada (a division of Pearson Penguin Canada Inc.) ·
Penguin Books Ltd, 80 Strand, London WC2R 0RL, England · Penguin Ireland,
25 St Stephen's Green, Dublin 2, Ireland (a division of Penguin Books Ltd) · Penguin Group
(Australia), 250 Camberwell Road, Camberwell, Victoria 3124, Australia (a division of Pearson
Australia Group Pty Ltd) · Penguin Books India Pvt Ltd, 11 Community Centre, Panchsheel Park,
New Delhi–110 017, India · Penguin Group (NZ), 67 Apollo Drive, Rosedale, North Shore 0632,
New Zealand (a division of Pearson New Zealand Ltd) · Penguin Books (South Africa)
(Pty) Ltd, 24 Sturdee Avenue, Rosebank, Johannesburg 2196, South Africa

Penguin Books Ltd, Registered Offices: 80 Strand, London WC2R 0RL, England

Most Tarcher/Penguin books are available at special quantity discounts for bulk purchase
for sales promotions, premiums, fund-raising, and educational needs. Special books or
book excerpts also can be created to fit specific needs. For details, write Penguin
Group (USA) Inc. Special Markets, 375 Hudson Street, New York, NY 10014.

ISBN 978-1-58542-937-0

Printed in the United States of America
1   3   5   7   9   10   8   6   4   2

BOOK DESIGN BY NICOLE LAROCHE

Some of the names and identifying characteristics have been changed to protect the privacy of the
individuals involved.

Neither the publisher nor the authors are engaged in rendering professional advice or services to
the individual reader. The ideas, procedures, and suggestions contained in this book are not
intended as a substitute for consulting with your physician. All matters regarding your health
require medical supervision. Neither the authors nor the publisher shall be liable or responsible
for any loss or damage allegedly arising from any information or suggestion in this book.

While the authors have made every effort to provide accurate telephone numbers and Internet
addresses at the time of publication, neither the publisher nor the authors assume any
responsibility for errors, or for changes that occur after publication. Further, the publisher does
not have any control over and does not assume any responsibility for author or third-party
websites or their content.

This book is dedicated to Benny and his brethren—every busted up, discarded, and caged cat, left waiting for the shining promise of home.

To anyone who has ever put their dreams on hold in order to make these lives more tolerable. Shelter worker, animal-control officer, foster parent, rescuer, feral champion, legislator—your sacrifice has meant everything.

And finally, to anyone who has ever adopted an animal, often decidedly averting their gaze away from the eyes of logic when a helpless one called out; thank you.

We are together the reason why animals will all have a home someday—and because of our efforts, someday will be sooner than we thought.

Preface

I'm a cat behaviorist.

In ninety-nine cases out of a hundred, when I say that, whoever I'm talking to says, "You're a *what*?"

"A cat shrink?" I try. Blank looks. "Cat therapist? Cat whisperer?" Nothing. "If your cat were peeing on your bed, I'd come to your house and help him stop."

Recognition. *Maybe*. And then, inevitably: "Can you really make a *living* doing that?"

"On a good week."

This was how I answered the reporter who wondered what I said when people asked me what I did for a living.

"Well, to be fair," she said once I finished, "you're not exactly what people think of when they imagine the Cat Guy."

She was right. I'm not. I'm pretty well covered in tattoos. My head is shaved. There are huge earrings dangling out of both my ears, almost down to where my beard reaches, which is normally just a bit north of my chest.

But it's okay, I told her, because it's all part of my plan. We need to explode the concept of what a cat guy looks like, what a cat girl looks like. We need a country literally *full* of cat guys and cat girls, bikers, politicians, clergy, and everyone in between, in order to keep millions from dying without homes.

I did this interview about a year before the premiere of my show, *My Cat from Hell*, on which I help people find ways to strengthen their relationships with their cats, using methods I started developing in the shelter where I worked and in whose trenches I learned how to love, appreciate, and work with cats on a higher level.

Since I began working with cats, I've met tens of thousands of felines, in shelters, in homes. But this book is about the one who taught me the most.

Benny was seven pounds of feline frustration who I loved with all my heart. I do not play favorites, and my house was always full of critters, but Benny *demanded* more than the others in every way. He was challenged physically and challenging behaviorally. He put me through my Cat Daddy paces for almost fourteen years and kept me humble while the larger world came a-knocking. When I moved from Boulder to California, I left the network of health professionals I had known before, so when Benny's health issues began to dominate the landscape I desperately reached out for new connections, veterinarians who shared my belief in an integrative approach. During Benny's first acupuncture session at a new local vet, I watched the way he almost seemed to melt beneath the well-placed needles. The doctor had a bedside manner, however, only marginally better than that of a potted cactus. I thought of blogging about the experience, but at that moment I realized my journey with Benny encompassed too much for a blog entry: growth, learning, setbacks, lessons in surrender and love. I wanted to write his story. Just like with *My Cat from Hell*, the idea is for viewers/readers to see the absolute most off-the-charts behavior, know there could be a way to salvage things, and look at their cat with renewed appreciation: "Well, *that* cat's issues rate a 10, and you're only a 6. I can handle that." I had no problem with the idea of presenting my little companion in that light. I'm sure he did. But then again, he had a problem with just about everything.

At the same time, Benny was witness to and participant in the most chaotic period of my life. I thought it important to talk about things that, quite honestly, I've kept exceedingly close to the vest. The thing is, I treasure beyond words the relationships I formed with animals in the past seventeen years. I find no drama in saying that without them, I would have long ago passed from this world. So in honoring them, I needed to reveal the dark corners they led me safely away from, despite my best efforts to hand grenade every single gift the universe placed at my feet. Benny was one of these animal ambassadors' toughest and most rewarding representatives. I am genuinely proud that we can share our journey with you.

Introduction

My relationship with Benny was long and tumultuous. A petite gray-and-white domestic shorthaired cat, he challenged me every day for more than thirteen years. Every time I let myself get complacent in my knowledge of cats, in my place in their world, I'd take a deep breath, lace my fingers behind my head and lean back in my chair, and look over to Benny . . . who was flipping me the bird.

Our story was one about two broken beings who fixed each other. His previous guardian, handing him over to me, called him "unbondable," even as he sat in a cardboard carrier, his pelvis shattered by the wheels of a car. I was an animal shelter worker, commiserating with and hiding among the only other beings I felt a part of. My life as an artist—a songwriter, singer, guitarist, bandleader, actor, performance artist; hell, my life as a vital human being—was being sucked from me.

Introduction

Having crawled out from the teeth of a nervous breakdown, I resorted to self-medication and a life of social and emotional solitude. For a time, my hermitage was a windowless warehouse with no phone, no running water. It worked for me. I was getting by, pissing in bottles, paying very meager bills, and, through an incredible array of addictions, staying necessarily numb.

Somehow during this time, I managed two things: my band and my growing empathic connection with cats. Believe this—I wanted nothing to do with developing a career working with animals. I just wanted the constant chattering in my head to stop. I wanted, as I wrote in one of my many unfinished twenty-minute-plus songs, "Peace from the Noise of the City." Just clean litter boxes, scoop poop, facilitate adoptions. . . . But instead I was becoming Cat Boy, the go-to source for what cats were thinking and how we could make their lives better while they stayed with us. Despite the sweaty layer of pharmaceutical shrinkwrap that muted my physical, spiritual, and psychological self, I forced myself to read, to study, to observe, to learn. Despite what I didn't want to be, something was growing.

And then, the first time I opened that carrier and met Benny's eye, my self-centered fantasy of living the indecently sweet life of one removed from humanity went poof. The challenges Benny presented throughout our life together were almost constant, whether physical, behavioral, or in that realm of ether that encompasses neither and both. Every day of my time with him I was either throwing up my hands, asking him for assistance, bouncing ideas off of other humans and other cats, just to get answers to bring back to him. He was aggressive to humans, felines, canines. He would decide to abandon litter box etiquette, seemingly on a whim. He would go on hunger strike. His body language and feline communicative skills were absolutely inscrutable. His shattered pelvis compromised him; his asthma was at times crippling; the still-mysterious ailments that took him finally brought me to my knees. And *that*, believe it or not, is a good thing.

I believe that without Benny, I might still have been successful as a cat behaviorist. But my experience with him brought me to a place where I had no choice but to abandon my comfort. For years I did OK living a life of disengagement. The things I believed kept me sane—strict cinder-block boundaries, addiction, cynicism, and self-sabotage—were unacceptable if I was ever to hear him. And if I was unwilling to hear Benny, I was unwilling to hear, learn from, *be with* every other cat in the world. I had to get clean of alcohol, drugs, and food. I had to accept humility. I had to be present and willing to learn and change. Things I would never do for another human (or myself) I did for the sake of Benny.

During his final months, he taught me how to die. I have

seen a lot of death. I have killed animals as a part of the world of animal sheltering. I have held countless others through the release of their animal companions and I have experienced it for myself. Benny wasn't done teaching me a thing or two even as his light flickered. I was at that point considered an authority on cats. And yet due to a combination of ineptitude (on the part of quite a few vets), stubbornness and a God complex (on mine), and continuing inscrutability (his), I was laid bare. Brought back to the person I was as a sixteen-year-old songwriter, throwing myself around the stage, singing my truth into the eyes of the audience until they had to look away. It took surrendering to the process of Benny's death to lift me spiritually and teach me what pain, loss, and love were about.

The day he died—actually, while I waited for the vet to come into that room and euthanize him—I told him exactly what his story would be; I'd write a book about how we co-healed, how we refused to let each other live broken ever after. And contained in that story would be practical advice: methodology and techniques specifically born from our time together. Maudlin as it may seem, I was committed to his living on. His level of difference allowed me to see the mind and body of a cat like I never had before. All cats—all animals, for that matter—took me to the water of understanding. Benny held me under until I drank. And now that I've come up to gulp some air, I want to tell you what I've learned.

Oversensitive
and the
Well-Dressed Demons

My game plan *felt* pretty ironclad. I would find the most autopilot-esque jobs conceivable. Barista. Pawn-shop employee and guitar buyer/seller. Landscaping (which, in the towns above Boulder, Colorado, at 8,000 feet, meant lugging rocks in a wheelbarrow from one end of a property to the other). Cleaning books-on-tape rentals with a damn toothbrush. I would have no investment in my work, other than to put a semihonest day in and get a paycheck out. Then, and only then, could I have enough creative fuel to imagine my songs during the day and flesh them out at night with my band, Pope of the Circus Gods. I remember when I was working for some bakery delivering baguettes at 4:00 in the morning, it happened: I was bundled up head to toe, since it was February and there was a gaping hole in the side of my van, and the words to one of my favorite songs came to me all at once, the tempo, I'm sure, in sync with the chattering of my teeth: *"In another story I would have waited up for her all night long/And when she'd finally pick my lock with my credit card I'd pretend to be asleep."* The chorus, with a sweeping, anthemic melody, came to me next, and as the sun cast her red spell over the Flatirons, my song "Notes from the Shed" was born. This was an unfathomable relief; ever since I had discovered that I was good at this, when I was eleven or twelve, I kept assuming the well was going to run dry sooner rather than later. So every time a song came to me in this way, I took a nice deep breath—I was still viable.

To be sure, there were many more mornings than not when this type of revelation didn't happen, but I hung my artistic hat on that particular dawn as proof that my plan *could* work. I was deluding myself. In reality, the Breakdown of six months before had sapped me of my mojo, and the ensuing cocktails prescribed to me made it almost impossible to access that deep, dark well that I had always relied on instinctually; in a cruel twist, that was exactly what the prescriptions were there for. Maybe it was that, maybe it was the increasingly desperate self-medication, but the end result was a reduction in life aspirations. My goal was just to get out of the mental rabbit hole I had fallen into and stay out. Writing was not so conducive to that, nor was an investment in life beyond the absolute minimum.

The problem was that I could never keep my ambitions too far in check. At the pawn shop, I became the dreamer—I had visions of turning it into Boulder's first classic and collectible instrument store. At the coffee shop it wasn't good enough to be a barista; I had to be an artisan, a roaster. Imagination and ambition were constantly colliding with the fear of insanity and the incredible quantity of substances I ingested in a desperate attempt to keep it at bay. If you've never rubbed shoulders with insanity, he is a sweaty, foul-breathed cab driver who locks the door and takes you wherever he wants. The more you squirm to get out, the happier he seems to get. Insanity loves—no, needs— company.

Once my short-lived career in the kitchen of a reputable restaurant died in a rockets'-red-glare moment when the bloody Band-Aid that slipped off my finger reemerged in a patron's mouth, I decided I was done with serving people. When I saw in the paper the next week that the Humane Society of Boulder Valley (HSBV) was looking for an Animal Welfare Associate, I took it as a sign; I would serve animals instead. My relationships from that point forward would be as pure as I could possibly make them. I was, after all, in search of simplicity. Write my songs, be with my band, serve the animals—I nodded vigorously as I ran this by my inner board of directors—a workable idea!

The funny thing about decisions based on signs or gut or visions is that they're usually nothing but noble outs. Just another way to sabotage yourself and keep your bigger life at bay. Beneath the nobility was a deep sense of emotional poverty; I couldn't afford truthful relationships with humans anymore. I was simply too beat up, too wary, too paranoid about where they would lead.

I walked in to interview at HSBV, therefore, after the restaurant, after the pawn shop, after the tape cleaning, after the rock carrying, more confident than I'd ever been at an interview before. My tattoo sleeves were just beginning to take shape but still, I felt I had no reason to hide who and what I was. My name was Jackson Galaxy—I liked big jewelry, I wore Elton John—ish glasses, and I had a head full of dreadlocks, dyed every color of the rainbow, with African trade beads and various and sundry other toys laced through them. Take me for my passion, I thought. Take me for my experience volunteering with animals (absolutely invented) and take me because nobody will scoop shit and pressure wash cages and care for the animals in your charge for very, very little money better than I will.

Audrey was the shelter manager. She was knowledgeable, driven but laid back, and hotter than July. I remember having one of those out-of-body events where I marveled that not only wasn't I nervous to be interviewing for this job, but I was flirting. Not overtly, not butterfly collar, gold chain, and cheap cologne, but just subtle enough to just make it seem like I was taken—but charmed.

When you're absolutely, positively convinced about the rightness of a fit, armed with the knowledge that the universe plopped you down like a UFO in Roswell for the sole purpose of making cosmic puzzle pieces seamlessly join together, you don't have to worry about coming off like a used-car salesman. As we spoke, there was never a need for anything with the subtext of "So, what do I have to do to get you into this beauty today?" while gesturing toward what used to be a beat-up 1974 Monte Carlo. When Audrey asked me if I had experience in a shelter setting, I just began to improvise a complete lie about my volunteer time at a New York shelter. I didn't think about Audrey doing her due diligence and calling; I was going to leave so little doubt that she would immediately skip the formalities and promote me to vice president.

"Do you have experience with aggressive animals?"

I pointed to my arms—imaginary points already covered in tattoos—"See this one? Akita mix. Kind of scary. But this one," I winced as I showed a group of freckles near my left wrist, "this really hurt. Believe it or not, a kitten. I'll take big-dog bite any day of the week."

"Agreed!" Audrey added emphatically.

Ever have a dream where you're walking, strutting almost, and you look down and you're on a tightrope? Suddenly then, you fight your balance with the 50/50 shot that you'll fall off. Well, in this lucid dream, I just refused to look at my feet, and nothing then affected my purpose, my strut, my vision of myself as Travolta on the Brooklyn streets in the opening moments of *Saturday Night Fever*. I worked the living shit out of that interview, even through the requisite warnings.

 Adopt, Don't Buy

Approximately four million cats and dogs will die in U.S. shelters this year. We've come so far by emphasizing the spay-and-neuter message, but we should be adopting the ones who need us instead of literally manufacturing more.

While approximately 30 percent of the animals that enter shelters are purebred, we as a culture still support mass breeders, commonly referred to as puppy and kitten mills.

We have two choices—to accept and embrace our role as guardians to animals or perpetuate a culture that deems them disposable. There simply is no in between.

"Jackson, we all are responsible for euthanasia here. I can't hire you if you are not willing to do that job."

"Of course—that's the only way it could be done. I can't imagine just shoveling that burden off onto one person. It's not fair, right?"

"So you're OK?"

"OK is relative. If I was completely OK with it, and I were you, I'd run the other way. But I get it, and with your help I'll get through it." This at least, by the way, was absolutely no line of bullshit. It was just projecting what it would maybe feel like. Audrey was giving me the numbers. At this point, in the early '90s, ten to twelve million animals were being killed in shelters every year. There were simply not enough homes. A no-kill world was not even an imaginable idea at this point to most, much less a workable goal, as it is today. Our job was to educate the public, push the spay/neuter message as hard as we could, and be there for the unfortunates. While we euthanized them. And that's what I told her.

"Animals come in here horribly abused and so traumatized that we can't save them."

I nodded. I swallowed hard as I tried to form words, an embarrassing nervous tic left over from a thirteen-year-old's first exposure to a large audience.

"You will be responsible for loading and emptying the crematory."

Again, a slow, wordless assent.

"You will have to assist or perform euthanasia at the owners' request with them present."

And then there was that hard-swallow response again. This was maybe the only time I looked at my feet on the tightrope that day; I was genuinely scared that I would have to try to find a vein while comforting both animal and human. It was hard to continue my Zelig-like projection into this tableau. I tried, though, as I sat there fumbling for a confident response.

"I'll be sort of mentored into this role?"

"Oh, absolutely. Until you can do it with relative ease, we don't want the guardian completely stressed out while you sweat the job."

"Phew. Good. No problem, then."

Audrey was fishing for bigger cracks in my good intentions. There must have been a flood of applicants like me during her tenure, inexperienced yet seemingly committed, who wound up folding like a cheap umbrella in a nor'easter. I, however, refused to give in, even though there were definitely moments where my fight or flight instinct had me out the door of that conference room and onto the street.

Ironically, it was the presence of the shelter mascot, a cat named Cheeks (so called because of his tailless status), that brought my blood pressure to a manageable place when Audrey's probing got me sweating. I would touch him as he paraded around the white laminated tabletop, cool to the touch in the summer heat, and he would just flop over, diffusing any tension dangling in the air.

At the end of any one of these moments, Audrey would ask, earnestly, "Are you OK with that?"

"I'm OK. I'm in. I want to be of service." And that was the truth, surprising the shit out of me as it came out of my mouth. What I couldn't see then was that, underneath the layers of shrinkwrap in which I'd covered myself, something in me really did want to experience life and serve someone else.

After an hour, the deal was all but sealed; Audrey took me on a tour of the building. While we were outside in the barnyard, looking at the pond, I asked when they were making a final decision; she said, verbally winking, "Oh, later today, I'm sure."

I went home knowing that my life had entered a new phase. This one didn't have the same "cool, I've got some cash coming in, rent and dealer will be paid" vibe of the other jobs. I just knew that there would be an actual emotional investment, and, despite intermittent spasms of fear, I was cool with it. The animals I had just visited, the dogs who licked my fingers through the bars, through the din of the adoption area, shrill barking echoes starting as one dog saw me, with the others falling like dominoes, the cats staring out from 2' x 2' cages assessing the threat level—all of them, I found instantly, speaking to me . . . I was still seeing them all as I drove home and, as I later told the people gathered in my house, I felt needed, I felt the call to service, and that felt good. It would save me. At any given time, there were up to a dozen people in our living room, band members and others. I was the elder statesman of the bunch. Passing the bong around the tribe, gathered nightly in a circle on our floor, serious as any council of elders, I knew everyone could feel it. My intent, my focus, my relief at finding a purpose heated up that room like a solar panel.

And then Audrey called me to tell me that I hadn't gotten the job.

"Really."

And there was zero sarcasm in that question; it wasn't even a question. I was simply stunned.

"*Really?*"

Usually I would have internally clocked out at that point, but I just couldn't. I was getting pissed. "I must have read that interview completely wrong."

"No, you didn't."

"Well, I . . ." My face was flushing an ugly red from the combination of anger and embarrassment at the thought of holding court, cross-legged like a big dumb Buddha, telling my friends that my life had taken a dramatic turn.

"No. Take my word for it. You didn't. We just need to go in a different direction."

"Which ... um ... direction ... would that be?"

Diplomatic pause, measuring what to say that wouldn't lead to an HR nightmare. "I'm sorry, Jackson. I hope you apply again."

"Oh. Yeah. Me, too ... umm. . . ."

Click.

What the living *fuck* had just happened?

I looked at the receiver and hung it up as if it were radioactive. I immediately felt concussed, sore, nauseated, and radically depressed.

I wandered semiconsciously around the house; up the stairs looking for a roommate, or drugs, or a roommate with drugs. Funny thing was that I had just left about nine people and nine cats sitting in the living room, downstairs, thirty-six eyeballs silently following my movements. When they saw me, nobody asked, because they all knew something really unfortunate had just bitch slapped me.

"Screw HSBV," I thought. "If they don't know the best thing that ever came their way happens to be a gift in wrapping they didn't like, then they don't deserve me." I was always a masterful self-saboteur/suffering artist. I would write a hit single and then stretch it out so it was thirteen minutes long, taking an amazingly catchy verse, chorus, and bridge and adding a goiter of a three-minute monologue that I would absolutely refuse to cut. Take me, all of me, or none of me.

I'm not sure when exactly I found out that it was my dreadlocks that cost me that job, but I got confirmation from the inside. Not getting to join those people and those animals in that organization took me beyond a place of just pissed off; I went on a serious bender. I was dangerously loaded for weeks. I had recently discovered a new cocktail: Klonopin (my antianxiety med) mixed with weed, cough syrup, mushrooms, and antidepressants. It was a crazy, hallucinogenic, totally mindless world to inhabit, taking me from amped to drooling in a predictable daylong sweep. I started "seeing" a girl, the sad memory of whom has burned through that particular blackout to live with me today (although her name is blessedly gone). We drank, snorted, popped anything we could find and, at some point in the night, had a few bumps of "break glass in case of emergency" coke so we could fool around without falling asleep midway through. We flailed in slow motion and kissed, our lips missing each other, kissing teeth or chin, laughing awkwardly but not self-consciously. The point of the black hole we created was to lose all sense of self while with another person so you didn't feel like crying in the middle of it. If I could have woken up just for a minute, I probably would have recognized that here was the point when "partying" became a collection of desperate measures, like trying to bail out a sinking boat with a jelly jar.

But I didn't wake up; I relied on the universe to take care of me, to not let me die.

For most of my life I have seen myself as eggshell-like, ill-prepared to deal with the gentle rinse, let alone the spin cycle. Others saw me, they repeatedly told me, as "oversensitive." I walked around for years like I was about to witness a car crash. When I was a child, my maternal grandmother, briefly a vaudeville performer and the only other person in my family with an artistic bone in her body (except rhythm—my parents met at a dance club and transcended their language barrier with some dance-floor-clearing moves), liked to tell me the story about how on the first night of her honeymoon in Niagara Falls she woke up in the middle of the night in a cold sweat and shook my grandfather awake. "Cy!" she yelled, gathering their belongings, "We have to leave right now!" And they did. He knew better, even as a newlywed, than to argue with her. And their hotel burned down to the ground later that night. She would tell me that we were made of the same psychic material—she could see it in me. (She was right in more ways than one; she was an addict and died of lung cancer from smoking. The last time I ever

saw her in her hospital bed, she touched my face and said, ·
"Everyone's going to try to get you to quit smoking, honey.
Don't do it!")

Although this oversensitivity jangled my nerves 24/7, it
also created an incredibly invested sense of wonder in the
human and animal condition. It made me almost predeter-
mined to be an artist and not, say, a CPA. There were things
I knew about you by watching you walk, watching your hips
move from across Broadway.

And then one day my Hungarian-born father brought
home this old Motorola record player, a big tweed box; you
opened the front speakers like a book and put records on
the turntable in the middle. He had gone to the nickel bin
at the bookstore and picked up random records, and I was
completely hypnotized. It didn't even matter what the songs
were. Of course once I discovered other 45s, my first being
the Jackson 5's version of "Rockin' Robin," I was hopelessly
lost in music. My parents were devotees of doo-wop and I
absorbed and regurgitated everyone from Dion to the Shi-
relles. I would put on a show every night for them consist-
ing of one song—usually "Chantilly Lace" by the Big Bopper,
complete with phone in hand as the song starts with a ring
and that lush baritone: "Hellooo Baby!" I now knew, before I
hit adolescence, what my life would be. Without the trappings of planning, without the trappings of worrying about
success, without the trappings of even thinking about fly-

ing too high and having my wings clipped or any of that, I understood that I would die with that Motorola around my neck.

As a singer (and, for that matter, as a writer, actor, and inveterate flirt), the oversensitive energy my grandmother saw in me served me well, because I could channel it into something useful. (It didn't hurt that my "something useful" came with the toy surprise of being able to yell at the top of my lungs. I have always been scared of shouting in real life. One of the reasons I walked away from acting and embraced performance art was that I was continually type-cast as a raving lunatic. But as a singer, I like to think, I ex-ploded the "sensitive singer/songwriter" stereotype into a million bloody little Dan Fogelberg–shaped pieces. Back-ground music I have never been.)

My life as a performer provided me with constant access to the feeling of high. I stepped onstage for the first time when I was not even a teenager. It was home, immediately. All of the frustration, the self-consciousness I felt walking through the rest of the world just faded away, ironically, when I stepped into the spotlight. My mom used to tell me a funny story about how I would walk down the street with her, decked out in Day-Glo colors, huge earrings hanging to my shoulders, glaring at everyone passing, and wondering loudly what they were staring at.

Once I discovered the guitar, I discovered songwriting.

They were almost simultaneous. And once I discovered songwriting, I had to play the songs for people. I didn't know that it had a name, but I took to busking on the streets of Manhattan. Money dropped in the case was a nice side effect, but, more important, I needed that urban version of white noise in order to concentrate. The attention I got was immediate. My observational skills got very sharp early, then sharper through college and acting grad school as I took theater into my embrace along with music. Whether it was my initial in—which was writing scores for productions—or then, as I obviously wasn't happy behind the scenes, acting, the methods, the questions asked, were the same. I would go to the park and watch people and ask: What is the inner life of these people? What happened in the moments before and after they make contact with me? Where are they going? Who have they left at home? Why does he lead with his chest and why does she slump her shoulders? From all the clues I gathered, I would make up a story that I could re-create in myself. It was all about investing your imagination in the story you created around these people (or, later, cats), and filling in the blanks believably and with high stakes.

It wasn't too long until I found other things that could bring the feeling of buzz and home without being onstage. I discovered weed soon after cigarettes, around the time I turned fourteen. Drink was actually always a distant second to other things, but it was more readily available. I'll leave out the boring and all-too-familiar story about what, where, and how; suffice it to say that there wasn't a buzz that I didn't want more of. The way young girls have dreams about losing their virginity to the man who would be the love of their lives, I had dreams about mushrooms, LSD, peyote. I would wake up with my heart beating as if I had just had a wet dream. Which, I suppose, I had.

Yeah, I was that kid. Everything tasted like more.

I kept my demons well dressed for quite a while. I was always a high-functioning addict. I didn't miss work, I didn't miss school. I kept writing music at a high level and never flaked on a gig. I held together various relationships, some with normies and some with fellow partiers. I finished college not as bad off as some friends, and I made it through grad school without too many hitches (unless you count my playwright classmates' always casting me as psychopaths a hitch).

However, by the time I moved to Boulder to be an artist and—finally!—a full-time singer/songwriter, I began to feel unsteady, glancing at my feet on the tightrope I had been walking for years. As a functioning adult, oversensitive served me not at all. I just never had the right amount of boundary to get through the world. Blessing and curse, right?

So many artist/addicts tell the same story: We used drugs

to help us reach new creative heights and to keep the high of being onstage alive during the more ordinary hours of the day. We also needed to shut the lights off at some point. Somewhere along that path, though, we lost sight and turned our chemical spirit guides into sledgehammers. Not to fall into the trap of artistic cliché, but you do have to access some deep, dark and unknown shit in order to get to the truth, to get from the point of looking through the cosmic windows of understanding to the point of *pushing through* them. And sometimes, before pulling the bullet out of your shoulder, you want an anesthetic shot. Inevitably, it becomes easier to be proactive about the shot. Bad things, things that are just too much to process or that you don't have the tools for, could be right around the corner—so why not be prepared for them ahead of time by staying numb? It's like the cat who patrols his home nervously and sprays the corners by the windows and doors. He figures that doing this is keeping the "outsiders" from invading, so he'd better just do it even though they haven't been coming around. Just in case they do, they'll know who this piece of the world belongs to.

When I landed with a thud in Boulder in 1992, I was barely holding it together; it only took another six months for me to lose my shit entirely. I was self-medicating heartily while working as many dead-end jobs as I could find to earn enough money for rent, dope, food (human and cat), and guitar strings. I was an idiot savant with a posse, letting others do my thinking and then blaming them for not doing it with my best interests foremost in their minds. In retrospect I see that I was surrounding myself with lightning rods, both human and chemical, rendering myself vulnerable to the inevitable ground strikes that eventually reduced me to a mass of exposed nerves, rocking incoherently under my covers and fully dressed, trying desperately every day to just get to work.

I was seeing a therapist and a psychiatrist, one to listen to me and the other to write prescriptions. I begged both to hospitalize me, just briefly, long enough to get my bearings. Instead, the psychiatrist led me down what was to become a ten-year rabbit hole of psych meds. Of course, like a good addict, I blamed her for all of it, the loss of everything I held dear. Never mind that the rabbit hole cost me everything, every human relationship, my band, my creativity—on the way down to the bottom, I was introduced to my best frenemy, Klonopin.

The miracle was that, though all of my artistic endeavors seemed to be lacking true humility—really, how does a rock and roll songwriter claim humility in the first place?—over the next several years, as my songwriting muse left me, she resurfaced in animal form.

. . .

When I read in the want ads that HSBV was hiring again, I was immediately nervous—butterflies in the stomach nervous—and simultaneously sad. The universe was rubbing my face in poo all over again. This provided all of the gross, unwanted emotion I needed to push my bender to all-time super-deluxe status. It was a scorching hot summer day, which, when coupled with whatever I had taken/drunk that day, made my sweat cold in the heat. I was standing almost buck naked on my balcony, playing my songs as loudly as I possibly could. I had three roommates with me, singing along. Across from us were the homecoming king and queen, tanning on their balcony. They were obviously not happy with the fact that I was drowning out the Phish soundboard jam they were tanning to.

"Really?" Barbie said. "Would you please?"

No answer, just that embarrassing-in-retrospect Chris Cornell/Robert Plant head nod, lost in dreadlocks.

"You're not even GOOD!" she shouted at me. She reminded me of the gig I had played to an empty house weeks before, save one table of girls who looked like her, absolutely tanked, interrupting me midsong so I would sing "Happy Birthday" to one of them. Remembering this made me sing and play even louder. I broke a string. I was completely out of tune and, I think, loving it.

"Jesus Christ," Barbie went on, incensed, "do you have to be such an asshole?"

I flipped her off. My roommates laughed extra hard and loud.

Then her life-size Ken doll stood up. I swear he turned his six-pack into twelve just getting out of his hammock. Using the breath from every pack compartment, he measured his words through his teeth: "Look, dude. I. WILL. CALL. THE COPS. IS THAT WHAT YOU WANT?"

And I snapped.

"This is what YOU want. You WANT. TO. Shut the *fuck up* or else I'm absolutely going to *burn your house down* and when you run out from the smoke I'll *punch you both in the face* and make you *cry!*"

I remember getting hoarse. My roommates were definitely not the kind to try to quiet down a confrontation, especially when loaded and in the middle of a Sunday when we actually had some energy. I screamed at Mike to get me scissors. Like a fool, he did. I swear I did this unconsciously in the moment, just to get a reaction and irreparably nauseate the doll twins, but looking back it was that moment of clarity. . . . I grabbed the scissors and cut off a dreadlock. I held it to my nose, feigned taking a deep inhale, and held it away in disgust like it was a sock worn three days straight in August.

And then I hurled it at them, hitting Ken right in the abs.

He screamed like a thirteen-year-old girl with Bieber Fever, and it was game on. I kept cutting, screaming obscenities, and hurling hair grenades. The perfect couple came gradually unglued, and every time it looked like they were going to score a point I'd hit them squarely with a big, braided, chunked-up, dyed orange or purple piece of hair that hadn't been washed for months if not years. They'd get grossed out and back away. Mike stood behind me and cut the rest off, like we were stockpiling snowballs for the big assault on our ice fort, and we all took a few and pummeled Barbie and Ken mercilessly.

Finally, it was over. I took a bow, left the stage . . . errr . . . balcony, went in, and shaved my head, which felt really amazing. Dreads tug at your scalp, and they have heft, especially with trade beads and coins and such in them (not to mention the occasional embedded twig). As I emerged, I felt different, lighter; still me, but somehow less of a human zigzag.

Again, retrospect is a genius part of the human-experience multitool—wear it on your belt with pride! I got to conform in the most rock and roll way possible. I was now buzz cut, yet I had done it with my freak flag flying proudly. "They" didn't make me cut my hair; it was just a radical part of making a completely forgettable drunken point.

I couldn't wait to go back to the shelter. "I was in the neighborhood" was, I believe, the unbelievable line of shit I fed Audrey when she looked at me, with a not-contained smile plastered on her mouth.

And this time, goddammit, that job was mine.

The Rapids,
the Monster
and the 45 Kisses

'm not at my best when the pressure is on and I'm in a new situation; it's the stuff actors' nightmares are made of. My first day at a new school in seventh grade was the first time I had encountered concepts like class schedules, periods, lockers, and, of course, combination locks, and the overload I felt was freaking me out. I was flop sweating my way through that day, and having spent eight minutes getting my locker combination wrong, I was busting ass to get books out for math class along with pencils, compass, protractor, and WHAM, I stabbed myself in the hand with a pencil, breaking the tip off. I wound up, after bleeding a puddle in front of my locker, at the school nurse, who told me I had nothing to fear, but said I had probably just given myself my first tattoo. I liked that she assumed there would be more. And she was right—I still have proof of my shaky embrace of things new and unfamiliar in the palm of my right hand.

My first day at HSBV was only marginally more successful. I was more hungover than usual—nervous about my new job (remember, I had lied my way in; I had zero experience as a shelter volunteer), I had made sure to take an extra helping of my cough syrup, weed, and red wine combination the night before just so I could sleep. Even though I had been given training materials and a step-by-step manual of how to get through the morning duties, the moment I walked through the door my seventh-grade panic button went off. On the positive side, I was kept so incredibly busy from that moment until 5:00 that my mistakes became a blurry comedy of errors.

Lesson learned. When you've passed out on the floor five hours previous and now you enter the lion's den, hundreds of animals yelling for food, banging through your skull like cartoon frying pans, it just gives you a gentle hint that you might want to modify your nightly rituals, or at least adjust the drugs of choice. And this all hits before the rest of your being is taken by the smell; dog areas, cat areas, and the barnyard are all very specific street corners in hell, scent-wise.

My first exposure was in dog adoptions. Allison was the

lead, the person in charge of putting me through my paces. And Allison could be on the short-tempered side, which I found out within minutes. I was already sweating. The room was large and acoustically unforgiving, with tiled walls and only small windows near the top of one far wall. A low wall made of cinder blocks divided the two long blocks of dog runs so that our residents wouldn't get into stare downs with a dog across from them. My recollection is that there were twelve long dog runs on either side of the half wall. These runs had metal dividers in the middle, which were used, when the shelter wasn't full, to guide dogs into one end so you could feed and clean on the other end. When the place was full, the divider also functioned as a wall, making two adoption runs.

On my first day, working in galoshes, shorts, and my green HSBV scrub top in the visible humidity and the equally visible stink and sound, I felt like I would crumble twelve times before lunch. It was as if the animals knew I was the new sucker on the block. Not only did I lose a few dogs out of their runs, tripping over my galoshes imagining a dog riot while they went parading to their neighbors and enjoying their infamy like Paul Newman in *Cool Hand Luke*, I also couldn't handle the multicolored nylon slip leads that experienced animal welfare associates used like tender lassos and wore over their shoulder and under the

opposite arm, giving themselves the appearance and bra-
vado of fourth-world generalissimos. The veterans of the
trenches I immediately identified and gravitated toward,
like Suzanne, Dustin, Kim, and even my feared trainer Allison, had a confidence in their movements, playing those
slip leads like violins, relocating dangerous dogs with catch
poles, "gloving" feral cats—these were talents I envied while
everything from four-leggeds to stainless steel bowls continued to slide through my fingers.

"Jesus," snapped Allison after I put my nylon slip lead on
wrong for the third time, "it's like you've never done this
before."

"Well, I—"

"Seriously. Whatever. Just get it right."

The rest of the day, blessedly, was a blur.

The first six months on that job were a complete whirl-
wind, physically, emotionally, psychologically.

Animal Welfare Associates trained in the back first,
working directly with the animals. We cleaned cages in the
morning, fed the animals, got the adoption area ready for
opening. Fast. Socializing with the animals, showing them
some love, was limited to the time spent as you relocated

from cage to cage, left a dish, picked up a dish. We had less than three hours between our drag-ass arrival and the opening of the adoption area, by which point every animal had to be cleaned and fed and the place made spotless. Spare moments were not to be had. Cigarettes were inhaled while running food out back to the pigs and roosters. Soon I started doing front-of-house work: taking in surrendered and stray animals, supervising visitations with guardians whose animals were being held by the courts for a variety of reasons, adoption counseling, matching people up with the right animals, and the very best part of the job—adopting our residents to new homes, getting them the hell out of that building.

At the end of the day, there was a circle of us who would convene at a coworker's home and do what we could to fix the damage the hours at the shelter had wrought. We had spent the day full of adrenaline, burning holes in our skin-colored thatched roofs. And now we had to chemically repair those holes, and try to glue our feet back to the earth. We would go to Lonnie's place—he was the front supervisor—and get copiously stoned, after which I would take a shower, because not long after getting the job I had moved into a warehouse with no running water, and then off to band rehearsal.

It really was an exhilarating time. I was no longer going to work just to take home a check—I was going to work to clean, to comfort, to keep spirits up, to find new homes, to help facilitate the human/animal bond, to learn about every animal that came under my roof, to protect, and to love.

But it wasn't just about learning to execute the job; it was about learning to execute it with compassion while also being comfortable—or at least OK—dealing with life and death on a daily basis. I cleaned and loaded the crematory, I believe, on my first day. I knew the smell of dead wildlife in my first hour. It was, after all, summer. Roadkill got ripe in a hurry.

Shelter work will teach you everything you ever wanted to know about trench warfare, keeping your focus on the immediate because any further downfield will drive you to distraction. Very soon after starting, you begin training to perform euthanasia. You're handling death right away because no shelter wants to invest time and energy in somebody who is going to burn out, so you might as well find out if the newbies are going to fall away quickly. It's so easy to dismiss shelter workers as automatons, heartless. Hard as it is to swallow, I've *never* met anyone as passionate, as unflaggingly "there" for the animals as the ones who show up day after day to care for and, too often, kill them.

The vet at the spay/neuter clinic where I cross-trained in my first few weeks was completely burned out, and she

really shouldn't have been practicing at a high-volume spay/
neuter clinic. I mean, I was a rookie, but you had to be blind
to miss her simmering resentment. I was helping with a
term spay (essentially an eleventh-hour abortion) of a lab
mix. There were something like six or seven puppies inside
this dog; the vet was pulling out the puppies in their embryonic sacs and I would then inject the embryos with sodium
pentobarbital, what we called blue juice. The embryos would
turn blue and then—this was fifteen years ago and I still remember what it looked like, I still remember the sound
the puppies made when they hit the stainless steel bowl. I
really wanted to prove I could handle this kind of truth,
didn't want to seem naive and ask a question like, "Why kill
puppies that would fly out the door as soon as they were old
enough?"

The vet started giving me a cold speech as I injected the
unborn pups, one she'd obviously given 1,001 times before:
"What's your name again?"

"Jackson." The sound of embryo on steel.

"OK. Jackson—" The contempt began to drip from the
corners of her mouth; she said my name as if it were the
name of the deranged uncle who smacked her around when
she was a girl.

"Jackson, this is what happens when people don't spay
their animals." A dead puppy embryo hit the large bowl

again. She used it as punctuation. And although I was mortified, as she went on my vague trembling began to take another shape—from nauseous fear to nascent rage. Trying to pull some Scared Straight shit with me. "I don't run a puppy mill, bitch," I thought to myself. "I'm one of the good guys."

I suddenly remembered the phrase that Lonnie had introduced to me as I took a hit from his two-foot ceramic bong just the night before: *compassion fatigue.* As far as I was concerned, this vet was the compassion fatigue poster child. I knew that no matter how long I worked with animals from that point on, she would occupy that picture in the pages of my inner dictionary. Lonnie told me that it was really common among shelter workers and, in his experience, would just sneak up on someone and bury them. Once you're just cleaning shit, processing paperwork, using embryonic puppies as punctuation marks—it's over for you. You care so deeply about the animals you serve, and you feel such empathy for them, and they never stop coming. There are always more. And eventually you can get to the point where you're all cared up, and you look for somebody, anybody to blame all of this suffering on. It creeps up on you, day by day, and you never even notice it.

I was obviously in no danger of burning out at that moment. I was on a semihysterical slide down the rapids, careening through a new life as an animal advocate as if it were actually mine. Of course there was a hidden branch, waiting to hang me from my belt loops—my enthusiasm, and the little lies that I inhabited like the world's best actor/salesman, were about to catch up to me in a big way. Euthanasia was something I had absolutely no experience with, and it was speeding at my head like a major league fastball.

When I saw my name on the daily E/C (Euthanasia/ Cremation) schedule, I was nervous as hell. As much as I was electrified by assuming the role of guardian, caring for a whole lot of somethings outside of my selfish existence, there was a lurking worry. In every corner of this building, death was standing and waiting, waiting for us to stop fighting and give in to the inevitable. I was face-to-face with my extreme naiveté. I was actually going to have to do it. I swore I would be an equal part of this tight-knit team, and euthanasia was what made us all equal. We were equal in the cold, damp eyes of the last house on the block, the heavy metal door that at some point had actually opened into the crematory but that, by the time I set foot in there, had been painted over scores of times. Now we had to sneak the animals we'd killed out the back door of the shelter, making sure no visitors joined us in the hallway, to put them in the crematory.

The first animal I assisted with was a dog—a bully breed, of course, a Pit-Lab mix; back then, as now, Pit Bulls and Pit mixes represented a disproportionate number of dog breeds killed in shelters. This one was scared and led to the room on a catch pole because he was found stray and unpredictable. In order to keep my shit even remotely together, I paid attention to tasks. Remember the combination to the safe. Take out the sedative. Remember the amount to give to a dog of his weight to "take the edge off." Wait for the edge to come off. We used a combination of ketamine and Rompun. One of the unnerving side effects of this cocktail was a disassociative state, a rhythmic hallucination that made the animals look side to side as if watching a tennis match. Talk to the dog. Be his advocate in these, his most treacherous moments. Keep your shit together. Fucking breathe, Jackson, rhythmic, even, slow, because even with the sedation he knows whether you're freaking, and if you are, he will, too. Draw up the blue juice. How much will it take? We weren't that far past the days when animals were killed en masse in decompression chambers or gas chambers; we were making up the rules in terms of comforting (did we do this in the dark or with the lights on? Alone or with people?). Learn restraint—gently bringing the head to the side, teeth away from the lead animal welfare associate who was injecting. Remember how to find a vein, roll it to the top of the leg. If not there, a back vein. In the course of my years there, I learned how to inject meds pretty much everywhere: IP (intraperitoneal cavity), IM (intramuscular), even heart sticks, when an animal was all but dead but a heartbeat was still present. I learned the angle of injection needed so as not to blow a vein. (This was the ultimate nightmare, especially when assisting with owner-present euthanasias. You do NOT want to have to find another vein in an elderly animal, causing him even more discomfort, while his guardian stands in front of you awash in sorrow.) What you wanted was peace for this animal. Yes, the concept seems absolutely sideways, but you do what you have to do in those moments. The Pit mix has his head and neck in my arms. Audrey injects. I feel him sigh and leave. Put him gently on the towel that's already below him. Spend a minute or so in silence, a habit I fell into from that moment on. Not really mourning for me, more like respect, giving him the time to settle into his new reality. It helped and helps me to see this life and death as transitional. I've felt the energy of this life leave so many times now that I really can't count. I've never once, though, taken it for granted, with my animals or the animals of others. That being said, I'm no monk; death sucks. Losing beautiful animals because of preventable reasons is a horrible and continuous ache, plain and simple. And my choice, slowly, became to not accept it. The job had to get done, and I would do it, but I would also do everything in my power to change the necessity at its source: I would commit to spreading a strong message about spaying and neutering, and I would work on shelter-based behaviors that I could channel. I could help keep these guys from slipping away in energy and spirit, which was, in most cases, what had led them onto the daily E/C list and into this, the last cold, damp room inside the last house on the block.

Which is why it hurt so fucking much the first time I had an "intellectual discussion" about euthanasia with someone at a party. He wasn't a shelter worker but, as he phrased it, "an animal welfare advocate." The discussion took a turn when he said, "In all of my experience, I've never met an animal who had to die in a shelter." Now, I'd had experience with someone calling me a Nazi; friends in other shelters had been called "robots," "heartless," "murderers," and obviously the list goes on. But here, it was as if something had been slipped into my drink when I wasn't looking. This was the most cruel of insults, one that was disguised in banter. I was dizzy and wordless. And in that stuttering moment, a grudge was born.

My good friend Lily, who was a volunteer at the shelter, heard about and became enamored with Best Friends Animal Sanctuary in the late nineties. She began donating a good deal of her money and telling people who were thinking of surrendering their animals to HSBV to perhaps instead consider taking the drive out to Utah to Best Friends, where all animals live their lives in the massive canyon that belongs to the organization, without the specter of euthanasia ever hanging over their heads. I was deeply . . . resentful? Jealous? Both, I'm sure. In my deep, dark psychic cave, I really wanted to work there. But a world where no-kill sanctuaries are the only models of sheltering animals was—and still is—a goal, not a reality. *Somebody* has to deal with the present victims of our throwaway society.

We're moving in the right direction. The number of animals killed in shelters every year is down from twelve million back then to four million today. But the fact is, as much as it saddens and sickens me to say this, the answer is yes, many of the animals in the shelter system that die every year *do* have to die like this, because there are still too many of them and too few homes.

I'm not, of course, talking about the population we refer to as community cats. They are our wild companions. We trap them, neuter them, and return them to their colonies. Their lives are decidedly shorter than others, but we don't make the decision to just round them up and kill them. They belong, just not in our homes. No, I'm talking about animals that are discarded, left to fend for themselves, those who perhaps escaped and were never relocated to their homes. Many of these animals wound up in our care incredibly fearful, unsocialized, and aggressive. We didn't have anything close to the space or resources to try to rehab these cases. The only choice is whether they die with shelter workers there who try to find a way to love them, or on the streets, diseased, injured, starved, uncared for, unloved, and alone. Even if the love we gave was fleeting, it was real.

When all great movements are in their infancy, they are nourished basically on the mother's milk of righteous indignation. It is a time of red-faced screaming and finger pointing. That's a good thing—we need to be angry to move toward any systemic change. But ultimately the fingers have to stop pointing and the hand has to get down to work—and that work is always messy. Now the no-kill movement has grown up, and organizations like Best Friends have a plan to change the status quo, not just rage at convenient targets. But there are still those who gather just enough information to make themselves dangerous and then froth at the mouth about what they deem the inherent negligence, incompetence, and, worst of all, apathy at kill shelters. These are the people who hurled epithets like "Nazi" at me and who do so to others in the field every day. Excuse me? Really? You're blaming all shelter administrators and workers for killing because they're, what, heartless and lazy? Sorry. Naiveté is one thing, but naiveté cloaked in righteousness is something else. So to all the people, then and (thankfully, fewer) now, who vilify workers in the kill-shelter system, scream-

ing about no-kill while doing nothing about the actual problem: fuck you. To the shelters who say you're no-kill so you
can get the donations but then turn away blind cats or
twelve-year-old dogs so that they don't mess up your numbers and you don't have to be the ones who euthanize them
when nobody adopts them: fuck you. To the people who
sneer at the euthanasia shelters for doing your dirty work
for you so you can keep your hands clean: fuck you. Twice.

The animal lovers who are our potential advocates need
not to be coddled and made to believe that their hard-
earned donations are making the problem go away. I'm not,
by nature, a finger-wagger. But throwing around the term
"no-kill" as the obvious and only answer was then, and still
is, an insult to the animals stuck in and the workers staffing
a broken system. Be angry at the system and do something
to change it. We worked with animals because we loved them
as much as, if not more than, most people. And every one of
us longed desperately to see a day when we didn't have to do
what we were doing. And if you doubt that one, well, fuck
you too.

Performing euthanasia was one thing; hearing the reasons people surrendered these soon-to-be-dead animals to

us, though, was a wake-up call of mind-bending volume. Seriously. A fourteen-year-old cat surrendered because a baby was on the way. Dogs with cancer given up because . . . they had cancer. It pushed our last buttons on bad days.

This guy brought in an adorable Rhodesian Ridgeback one day and my friend Martha did the intake.

"I'm really sad to have to give him up," said the guy.

Martha slipped the shelter lead over the dog and knelt down to rub his chin. "Why can't you keep him?" she asked, standing up to lead him back into the kennel.

"I'm moving." Martha froze.

"Where the hell are you moving to, China?"

She didn't last much longer at the shelter.

On these days we reminded ourselves—indoctrinated thinking from early on—that at the very least, these people brought their animals to us, instead of just turning them loose in the street or abandoning them in an empty apartment. This happened and happens with astounding regularity. I have to say, my education in how the world at large sees and treats animals was far more depressing than the act of killing the unfortunates. I was just the messenger. The message came from a place that had decided not to value any sentient beings that didn't speak and walk on two legs. How could this not inform the choices I made regarding what I considered my new sense of purpose? Holding a stray dog, being his *guardian* for those last minutes, cradling him, and letting him know he was loved, trying to will him into dying knowing nothing but a life full of love. I knew I was doing the upside-down world more good than bad.

There was no such thing as an average day at the shelter; I could never afford myself the luxury of leaving home and thinking, "Okay, my day is going to look like this." I had come from a job where I was putting a toothbrush to an audiobook rental box for eight hours a day. At HSBV I was more engaged, more in the moment—anything could and often did happen. One day, after Pope of the Circus Gods played a late-night house party gig on the Hill, the epicenter of college life in Boulder, I slept through my alarm. This was a relatively easy thing to do living in a warehouse—there were no windows, just the massive bay door. The things that woke your ass up if the alarm didn't were your bladder and the mountain sun beginning to beat its oppressive song on that metal. When you woke up having to pee and with no running water, you either grabbed a bottle or made a dash for a hidden outdoor location, stopping on your way for sunglasses so the adjustment wouldn't make you grab your head in pain. This was before cell phones, but we had no landline anyhow. I was absolutely isolated from the world. When I realized what had happened I just tore ass into work, because for once, I really cared if I got fired. It was only when I got inside that I realized that I had managed to run from the warehouse to my car, drive to the shelter, and run across the dirt-and-rock driveway with no shoes on. Going back home would have put everybody's morning routine behind, so I just worked the whole day in the huge, one-size-fits-all rubber boots we wore over our shoes when we were washing kennels, making slapsticky fart sounds every time I took an increasingly sweaty step. Commitment to something outside of myself, my immediate needs—who got fed, who saw my face, who got their meds and attention from me, and who I could finally send to a home—was a *very* new feeling.

It wasn't as if I knew I'd discovered my true calling in taking care of cats. I never, not one time in my life, identified myself as a "cat guy." Let's just get that out there. I grew up with a dog, got my first cat in college, but managed never to be owned by one until grad school. Even then, it wasn't like I felt this calling, this "aha" moment of life-purpose recognition. That dance ticket had already been punched by music very early in my life.

I did, however, recognize a distinctly dogcentric culture

pervasive in our shelter and others that I visited. Not that it was an intentional feline snub, it wasn't as if we loved cats any less; dogs were just so much more understood, and thus more "reformable." We had dog training for volunteers aimed at socialization for faster adoption. We had volunteers taking dogs for long walks on the winding trails behind the shelter. The shelter was full of dog-enrichment opportunities.

The cats, not so much. They were in single stainless steel cages, surrounded by potential threats in the forms of fleeting fingers, feet, and scents. The volunteers who loved cats had nowhere like a winding trail to bring them, so they were mostly brushed in their cages or brought into a spare meeting room. This did little to relieve the anxiety the cats felt at the sensory overload. Unlike most of the dogs I've observed, kennel-crazy cats retreat: turning their backs to the bars of the cage, hunkering down in litter boxes, digging into blankets, trying to hide in hiding places that aren't there. The potential adopters, who spent an average of four seconds in front of a cage, would interpret their behavior as sad—and who wants to adopt a sad cat? Every cat who refused to look at visiting potential pet guardians became a cat who was euthanized needlessly.

That "sadness" was the impetus toward a new path for me. I began to see my "in" as affecting cat behavior, sure,

Cat Mojo 101

Environmental enrichment is crucial for the well-being of your cats. Let this be your initiation into the world of **cat mojo,** or how to see the world through cat-colored glasses:

1. Cats need to hunt. Play and prey is the same thing. If your cats don't hunt, they don't own their space; so play with your cats in an interactive way. Take them through the process of "hunt, catch, kill, eat." EVERY DAY.

2. Cats need to own territory. They do this by scent and visual marking. Make sure they have plenty of soft beds, blankets, scratching posts, and the like and put them in territorially significant places—i.e., places that smell of you!

3. Cats see every room in 3D: It's not just about the floor. It's the floor, the couch, the barstool level, the sink, the bookcases. Having access to all aspects of this world creates another level of territorial security.

but also in the momentary human projections that could signal "my cat" versus "not mine." One look, one step toward the front of the cage, a paw reaching between the bars to make contact. I began reading everything about cat behavior I could get my hands on. I ate up every word. And I'm telling you, for a guy who doesn't like to read anything without pictures in it, this was a hell of an accomplishment. And when I read something about cats, I could immediately walk into the back and observe that behavior. My earliest experiments with play therapy and positive reinforcement came by working with cats who had been going so kennel crazy that they were on the euthanasia list. I just took them after hours and experimented with what kind of play worked best for them, or how to get them through the theories of operant conditioning, using clicker training, to give me that high five through the bars that made them stand apart so well in adoptions, or at least walk to the front of the cage. And upon getting an answer with one, I experimented with another. Everybody won. Even Cheeks, the shelter mascot, became a test case, though it meant I started getting into arguments with some of my coworkers. Chasing the vast horde of mice who lived in the shelter's walls and, yes, eating them would help his diabetes, I insisted every time somebody tried to get him to stop by prying mouse parts from his clamped jaw. I began to enthusiastically turn that attitude around, insisting that coworkers, volunteers, and, really, anyone within

Cats CAN Be Trained!

Clicker training is a training system based on positive reinforcement and has been used on animal species from whales and dolphins to chickens, pigeons, cats, and dogs to great effect (see *Clicker Training for Cats* by Karen Pryor). While I'm not a fan of using this great tool to teach tricks that seem humiliating to animals (i.e., jumping through hoops or riding bicycles), clicker training can be used to

1. achieve a desired result to help you get along better with your cat, e.g., perform a sit while you prepare dinner;
2. emotionally connect with your cat by having a structured activity;
3. combine the two in cat agility training, which exercises a cat's mind and body, while strengthening the bond between the two of you.

earshot *watch* Cheeks transcend his illness and enjoy life as the raw cat that he was.

That was when I found a deeper level of cat recognition than I had ever seen in myself before. I knew not only *that* they were sad, for lack of a less-anthropomorphic word, but I knew *why*. The dogs in our care threw those feelings out toward the shallow end of the psychic pool. No offense to the dogs; in fact, just the opposite—dogs know how to make humans respond. Dogs have socially coevolved during their trip with humans much the same way humans have with other humans. This, of course, is a fancy way of saying that they know how to push our buttons. This was never, during the evolutionary timeline of the domestic cat, a concern, so it was never a talent they cultivated. But I began to feel that when I looked at any cat in my care, a conversation began.

Let me explain before another word is written: I have never once asked a cat, "So tell me what's up, Charlie?" and Charlie says, "Jeez, Jackson, thanks for asking. A little annoyed by the fluorescent lights, and will you please check out this tiny piece-of-junk pan I have to crap in but, hey, I still got my legs, you know? Can't complain, pal."

What is an animal communicator anyway? The definition of communication is: *The imparting or exchanging of information or news; the successful conveying or sharing of feelings or ideas.* So, do I communicate? Of course I do. It's the only thing I have, save the performer-to-audience nirvana, that reminds me of the holy, the stillness that others have described to me in respect to their meditative practices. With every blink, every exchanged subtle nod, widened or constricted pupils, we feel each other vibrate. You hold your breath, I hold mine. If the hair is standing up on my arms, so is it on your body thirty feet away. I raise my chin three inches, you relax and know me. You plaster yourself against the wall under the headboard, I find myself starting to cry. Neither of us is more or less than the other. Communication is understanding, slowing time and space down to the common denominator that is the spiderweb strand connecting being to being. And *that* has nothing to do with language as we know it. English, as it pertains to *this*, is not only ridiculously beside the point, it's our enemy.

So with that, the one splinter in my side in terms of my relationship with my clients is the pressure I feel from them to explain what their cats are feeling, and when I can't, they often get disappointed and frustrated. I can interpret motions, changes in energetic temperature—but the rest simply can't be outsourced. I'm not trying to withhold from you, to gloat over knowing your cat better than you; I just can't tell you in English what your cat is saying in Cat. I want you to meet me in these cool dreams. They are in no way exclusive. If I am anything, it's maybe the kite that introduces lightning to skin. I can't—nobody can—breathe life into the animal experience with air from the human one, and maybe that's where the two-legged companions get impatient and look for a shortcut. So when I spend alone time with a cat, upon reentering the human atmosphere I never know how to answer the question, "What's Ralphie thinking?"

At the time, of course, I hadn't really thought any of this through; I just knew I wanted to be the advocate, the steward that I knew I could be and I pushed so many others to be. And I knew I couldn't communicate "cat" to humans without being armed with human-type vocabulary, studies, and such. I could have screamed to the hills that I had some sort of deal struck with the cat world, but with my name and the tattoos and beard I seemed crazy enough already. I knew I needed to be balanced with a degree of legitimacy if I wanted to make a difference.

Within a couple of months I had been promoted to front-desk supervisor. Seriously, go figure. Turnover at that position was pretty damn high, because it was a job built for burnout; working at the shelter was hard in any position, but the front-desk supervisor was the one who got to deal with the people part of the equation—dropping off the animals they'd had for twelve years because "there just wasn't room anymore," for instance. Many of us came to the shelter because of our respective levels of human burnout. Getting put at the front desk meant you had more of that diplomatic *je ne sais quoi* than the others, which was truly a backhanded compliment. The pressure at that desk was palpable. The supervisor at that time, Lonnie, was like the valve on a pressure cooker. He diffused difficult situations expertly and calmed us pretty brilliantly as well. It was obvious, though, that it was beginning to get to him. Going back behind a closed door and kicking holes in the drywall or the copier. Then he started spouting off at me and other coworkers. One day, the pot blew the top clear across the room. He absolutely exploded at something, however inconsequential and camel's-back-breaking it was, threw papers in the air, and literally walked out. On his way out he took the master cash-register key, hanging like the front-desk crown on a lanyard around his neck and whipped it, I'm sure unconsciously, smacking me in the back of the head with it. Lonnie has left the building. Thank you, and good night. The next day my friend and I, hired in the same week and with less than six months of experience each, became cosupervisors.

Everyone knows the feeling, or at least I hope they do— I'd hate to be alone on this one—you get to a destination and it's . . . not *it*. The job you wanted, the apartment you wanted, the city you wanted. You wake up one day, and you say, "Boulder. That's the place. That's where my creative peaks will be hit and that's where I'll be inspired and the people will move me and I will love the mountains. . . ." You don't even have to see the place. You figure that you will reach personal peaks in the land of peaks. And if you don't, well, it's as safe a place as any to have a nervous breakdown. After living in your car for a summer so you can afford the move, after literally and figuratively investing everything, one morning you look up at your snowcapped neighbors in deep but removed admiration and look back at yourself and say, "This. Isn't. *It*."

Well, this promotion was one of those *its* that it wasn't. This was a ton of paperwork, a ton of headaches. I hated being an administrator. We had to turn people down for adoptions. We had to collect large sums of money from people whose animals had gotten lost and subsequently been impounded. I gingerly guided more red-faced, neck-vein-bulging, spit-hitting-me-in-the-glasses people than I can count into a conference room so as to avoid a domino-effect mass tantrum. Sure, we also facilitated adoptions, we made sure the fit was right; we did a lot of positive work. But I felt the pressure cooker churning. I was not in any way a confrontational person, so I began to dread the angry ones, and of course my oversensitive self could spot them the instant they walked in. I did my best to use my verbal aikido skills to take negative energy and throw the offender off guard by letting it pass through me, but I could only do so much.

"I don't *believe* this!" a guy started screaming at me one day when I told him he was going to have to pay us to get his impounded Corgi back. He looked around—the counter was three deep on an especially busy Saturday—like he was trying to get a posse together. The crowd was big enough that I couldn't speak in my reassuring jazz DJ voice.

"But, sir—"

"You'd rather put my dog in the *gas chamber* than give him back to me!"

His ticket was fifty dollars, and he was wearing a Rolex that clearly cost more than I would make in the next two months. "I don't think—"

"You Nazi *fucks!*"

And I blew. I lost it. I pulled a Lonnie. I dove over the desk to grab him by the neck. Luckily, he took one step back and I awkwardly landed on the floor. My coworker guided *me* into the conference room and I sat there, recalling the day I interviewed with Audrey in that very seat not six months earlier. I had completely crumbled in such a short amount of time, and with my mental state already in such a precarious place, I knew it was time to say that *this* wasn't *it*. I needed to move forward. I had to know what bigger purpose I could serve.

I started spending a lot of time with Daisy, our Community Outreach Coordinator, who had a gift for educating people without talking down to them. As opposed to the "teaching" demonstrated by the burned-out spay/neuter vet, Daisy was genuinely excited by her job, by her role as animal ambassador. When she spoke to me about taking "boots to the pavement," it was with a smile and enthusiasm so encompassing that her skin would flush in blotches on her face and chest. She took our message of compassion to the public at a time when the People for the Ethical Treatment of Animals was one step away in the public eye from terrorists. Daisy brought our ideas about spaying and neutering and anticruelty into classrooms, expanding the message of compassion from a starting point of domestic companions to *all animals*, sometimes using graphic, undercover PETA videos. We're talking sixth-graders, tenth-graders; we're talking children to whom you could bring a new perspective at a very critical time in their lives. Daisy and I spoke often about the concept of stewardship—we are not "owners" of animals in the same way that we are owners of lawnmowers and book bags. We are stewards. We are their guardians. Daisy, more than almost anybody else in those days, shaped the core of my understanding of our job in relation to the animals with whom we share the world.

Daisy was way too karmically correct to explain why she had decided to leave, but it was a done deal before the gossip machine could even start to spin. Regardless, when she said to me that she was leaving, I immediately wanted to honor her by continuing her job. The problem was that actually coordinating—unsurprisingly, an important part of the job of Community Outreach Coordinator—was a little beyond me, as I had begun to demonstrate with my fragile grasp over the front desk. Per usual, though, that didn't stop me. I figured my intensity, my beliefs would make up for my distinct inability to organize.

So, as I had done originally at HSBV in just getting a job there, I acted "as if." I squeezed into the clothing of Outreach Coordinator at HSBV, and convinced my superiors that it was a perfect fit. In many ways the formfitting suit highlighted my natural gifts. Theater is my home, and I was a natural at anything performance based; that is to say, I talked the shit out of animal welfare, spaying and neutering, our role as guardians, the mission of the Humane Society, from elementary-school rooms to boardrooms and all places in between. My ability to connect with an audience from the stage transferred easily into rooms full of children, corporate suits, the press, or whoever I was with on any given day. I knew what they could digest and tolerate as if it were printed on a page in front of me, and I played to those places and pushed their fences to almost bursting but not quite. I got the message across in ways they had never heard (or felt).

But my mind doesn't work in organized ways. My mind works in spurts of ideas. If someone or something is around to catch the spurts, all the better. But more often than not it's just me, and then the ideas all slip down the drain, which meant that I absolutely sucked at projects that required long-term concentration and planning. I could envision the final appearance of, say, a twenty-minute PowerPoint, but the execution of said presentation was just this side of impossible. If my attention span was challenged in any way, I could find myself in an hour-long quest at Office Warehouse for the perfect-feeling fountain pen by which my project would live or die. All respect to the administration, because they hung in there with me. They brought in a professional organizer, they hired an assistant for me, they gave me all the time in the world to accomplish goals, and they didn't tighten the screws until they felt like I had left them no choice.

But even as I did (some of) the job of Community Outreach Director, it was when working with the cats that I felt most at home. And then I crossed a threshold.

On that June night at about 2:00 a.m., I was where I would always be with a deadline looming; cold sweating my coffee at the shelter face-to-face with the familiar and sad realization that if I wanted to keep this position, I had to do my work when distraction was at a minimum. The eastern part of Colorado had been dry as a bone for what seemed like forever, and now we were getting some serious weather. The rain pounding the roof frightened me, because the shelter was actually right in the middle of a flood plain, and if the rain got too heavy on ground that was as thirsty as it was that night, we would be in some major shit. Inspiration for this presentation had run aground and I was subsisting on pure will at this point, knowing that every passing minute meant another half hour of lost sleep and that much more "up" drugs I'd have to do in the morning just in order to get to this place tomorrow. And to top it all off, there was the noise. The echo in our building was this side of torture—on a night like this, with the rain and thunder crashing, all you had to do was walk ten paces in any direction to catch the desperate pleas of the different holding areas; if I had to pee then I'd catch the dog impound area; to the soda machine, dog adoptions; the copy machine, cat adoptions; and just sitting at my desk, staring at the growing water stains in the corner of the ceiling, feeling the creeping clamminess of too much coffee (and other stimulants) and too little sleep, the cherry on top was cat impounds.

They. Were. *Screaming.*

In my highly agitated state I understood why new parents need to count to ten so they don't shake their babies. I knew we had a few new moms and litters. We had taken a transfer of cats from another shelter helplessly bursting at the seams in the aftermath of kitten season, plus our normal load of strays and "owner surrenders." They were all screaming; the noise from the rain and the barometric shifts had riled them up, and the worse the weather got, the worse the cats got, because they had to voice their anxiety somehow. I could feel my blood pressure surging to the point where my ears were ringing more than normal. (I had long ago developed severe tinnitus from my earplug-defiant performing.) I remember my head hitting the desk in final exasperation. When I raised it back up, it was with a plan.

Anitra Frazier, from my hometown of New York, was one of my first "remote mentors." In my new cat endeavor I was pretty shy and lacked the self-esteem necessary to make the phone calls to the precious few others established in my field, so I read their books instead, voraciously, having imaginary conversations with those who shared my thinking. Anitra seemed to me to be the Mary Poppins of holistic cat thinking. She went from consult to consult on a bicycle through the streets of my childhood neighborhood. She worked with multiple modalities and wasn't afraid to fuse behavioral know-how with the unshakable confidence that her empathic instincts were *right*.

One of the concepts Anitra brought to light was the "Cat I Love You." She walked down Manhattan streets, she wrote in *The Natural Cat*, going from brownstone to brownstone. She'd reveal her face to the cats lounging in the midday picture windows and, to introduce herself in a nonthreatening way, greet them with a slow blink while thinking the words "I love you."

When I first read about this trick, I had immediately tried it on Velouria, one of five cats living with me at the time. And it worked—just like Anitra had predicted, Velouria returned the blink and visibly relaxed.

The importance of the Cat I Love You, and the variations on the move that I was messing with, cannot be overstated. This is our "in" as humans into the communicative world of cats. They reach out with many of their vocalizations, which were obviously designed for humans. Cats do not meow at one another, by and large; they use it for us, to get something *from us*. So when you think about it, we owe them an attempt to listen, even when it means hopping to their side of the communicative fence.

As a cat behavior newbie, I thought that the Cat I Love You could very well be the feline Rosetta Stone. Almost hysterically tired and stressed out as I was, my idea was to put everything else aside—sleep might not happen tonight but for a few sweaty spurts with my head on my desk, and the presentation might not get done—but unless I got the cats to quiet down, it was all going to hell anyway, so I might as well experiment a bit.

I step toward cat impounds; moments later, a huge thunderclap scares me into the room. And as if they aren't already screaming, every cat in the room steps it up to 10 in response to the thunder/human presence one-two punch. I turn the light on—a mistake, I realize a moment after I do it, because there are no windows nearby and the cats think it is morning and time to get fed. So they turn it up to 11.

I count forty-five cats. The room is a small square, maybe 14' x 14', but the banks of stainless steel cages around the perimeter make it seem even more intimate. I decide I don't want to wind up painting myself into a corner; in case I happen to calm a cat down, I don't want to chance walking past her cage again and reenergizing her. So I start at the bank of cages closest to dog impounds. Which, you know, is great. The dogs can smell me through the rickety swinging door and they start the cascade of manic verbal dominoes. This is going to be like navigating a room full of armed mousetraps. I'll start high right, go left, then a row down and right. This is, by far, the biggest challenge my fragile focal span had to face. Ever. How do you pay attention to one tree when the whole forest is *screaming*?

Nevertheless, I take a deep breath. I step forward. I come face-to-face with a shorthaired tuxedo-patterned cat. Eyes opened but lazy: "I"—slowly closed, "Love"—and open again, "You."

Nothing.

THE CAT I LOVE YOU

Anitra's Cat I Love You isn't just for cat behaviorists. Try it yourself. First, look at your cat. Soften your gaze, remove all challenge to his perception. This is important: understand the difference between staring and soft eyes. Then match an eye blink to the silent phrase "I love you" like this:

1. Eyes open— "I"
2. Eyes fall slowly closed— "love"
3. Eyes open again slowly— "you."

If you're truly relaxed and your intention is focused and genuine, your cat will respond, first by blinking—and then by relaxing, dropping his guard just a tiny bit.

"I."
"Love."
"You."
Screaming.

Deep, cleansing breath. Frustration out. Healing intent flowing through me.

"I."

"Love."

"You."

I want to soothe you, goddammit, can't you feel that?—*I will heal you whether you like it or not!*

Wait, Wait, no, that doesn't work.

"I."

"Love."

"You."

Pause. Breathe. Do it again, Jackson. Believe your words.

And then I realized: He may be a cat but he's an audience. Convince your audience of your desire for them. . . .

"I."

"Love."

"You."

There. There it is. Not a blink back but a pause in his terror, a relaxation in his eyes. His pupils suddenly not so dilated. . . .

"I."

"Love."

"You."

(And the newly added cleansing breath.)

Finally, as if I've not necessarily made a friend but worn

down my friend's enemy, he slowly returns the blink. No more does he look for an escape route. His fight/flight mechanism alarm bells are finally reset by the promise of security that my eyes have brought.

"I."

"Love."

"You."

Easier now. We are officially cool. I desperately want to reach out and complete the new understanding with touch, but my instincts as a teacher inexplicably emerge to outweigh my simplistic emotions. I have a job to do; one down, forty-four to go.

I'm hooked in, and the feeling reminds me of that seemingly long-ago morning in a ripped-up panel van delivering baguettes in the middle of Colorado February, sunk into my source and writing a song that my forefathers would be proud of. Time slows and choices are all right. If they aren't they can be discarded with ease and lack of personal attachment. They are fruit from an everbearing tree. The difference is that here I'm not dealing with melody, tempo, story, and the almighty chorus; here I'm dealing with an unfolding language, where I have uncovered a few precious words in common. The rain isn't letting up, and I have to let everyone know that if they allow themselves to trust me, I won't leave them and it'll be OK. Have faith in me; see my relaxation in the face of potential danger and mirror it back to me.

The night slid along like an acid trip, sometimes peaceful and sometimes harrowing but all part of the same singular thought. My job was to smooth out the room and demonstrate peace through "I" "Love" "You." I remember at one point stripping down to my underwear because I was tied to these clothes now for the next working day, and I didn't want them to be as wet as I was making them. I also liked the freedom of being alone with cats, finally completely unselfconscious. I spoke in different silent tones from one cat to the next, from old to kitten, from solo to mom. I was present with each individual. As soon as I began to take my burgeoning process for granted, the next cat would bitch slap me into submission again. With renewed humility, I'd move on to the next.

How long was it? All I know is that when the room was "suddenly" silent, I slid down the wall, completely spent. Reveling in the quiet, I noticed the sun coming up outside my office window. It had been hours. There was a moment where I felt some of the forty-five cats sitting in their glorious silence, as confused by the outpouring of mutual support and newfound lingual skills as I was.

I found the energy and the focus to finish the presentation even as the crew poured into the shelter a few hours later to begin feeding and cleaning. There was motion all around me, but I found the slowness that one also finds in meditation. And when dealing with cats in general, or cats one by one, that slow reality is absolutely invaluable. Cats can fall into a zone while watching birds—fully immersed and engaged in the "activity" but conserving energy until they seem, for all intents and purposes, completely still. That night I met them at frantic and helped guide them back into their most natural state of confidence and stillness. The gift for me was the inner-body knowledge of what a confident cat looks like. Even in a cage, even without possessing a grain of territory, without a family or any place to go besides a 2' x 2' cage, cats can still exude confidence. Getting the cats to that point not only helped me in a very selfish way, I believe it provided them with another important thing—feline confidence, what I refer to today as "cat mojo," that one little oomph that a lot of these guys needed to navigate life at a shelter somehow intact, that helped them present in such a way that they simply went to new homes faster.

When you are blessed enough to have a defining moment, you are doubly blessed if you have the presence to appreciate it as such. For me, however, no defining moment came without the vision of that old double-barrel shotgun loaded with fear and doubt. "This isn't what it's supposed to be like," I thought. If I ever claim to walk a walk, I knew, then I had a fucking obligation to *this*. "Dammit! . . ." I hissed. It felt like a moment during a short, meaningless fling when it suddenly shifts; the kiss feels blissful and familiar, like you've done it millions of times before, maybe in another life . . . "don't go there, don't let it happen . . ." and against your best bachelor judgment, you separate slowly and lock eyes. And, goddammit, you are hopelessly in love. Defining moments are surely blissful, but, if you are stubborn enough, like me, to still believe that this life will unfold according to your *plan*, they are just as starkly terrifying.

Regardless, the universe was gentle with me as it asked me to appreciate both the blessing and the feeling of being completely screwed. And I did. And I do all over again every time I tell the story of the forty-five kisses, or now as I sit here at 3:00 a.m. in a wholly different state of mind, fifteen years down a very bumpy road, writing about it. Those cats, wherever they may have wound up (those kittens are now seniors!), gave me a gift.

Thank God, because, given what was about to happen, I was going to need it.

Omni Presence

Fostering is one of the most rewarding experiences there
is," Stephanie was saying to the hundred or so new volunteers assembled for our monthly orientation, when the
shelter staff tried to excite volunteers about ways to get
involved in shelter work and animal care. Stephanie was
our foster care coordinator, and in the three years I'd been
working at the shelter I'd come to love her because she
cared about caring. She understood that a growing and energized core of foster parents was the cornerstone of our
true goal, reducing euthanasia of adoptable animals. The
rest, the politics, she let slide over her.

At this point, however, the baton had been passed from
coordinator to coordinator for over an hour; waiting for
my turn to talk about community outreach, I was well into

my smile-widely-while-your-eyes-glaze-over phase. In and out of focus, I took in the glaring whiteness of the room. I'm sure that was the only reason I was awake. It was positively institutional.

"We wouldn't urge you to foster if we didn't put our money where our mouths were. Everybody on this staff has fostered." I noticed a few random pencils in the ceiling, and the cartoon pleas for children to learn the classics (we rented space in the public library for these gatherings). "Bridgette, the shelter manager, has fostered; Sarah, our volunteer coordinator, whom you've all talked to, has fostered; Jackson, our outreach coordinator, has . . ."

No no no no no no no no no!

"Jackson has . . ."

My eyes bugged out as I glared the *ix-nay* glare at her.

"Um, Jackson, have you ever fostered?"

I muttered under my breath, hoping she'd interpret it as, "Of course I've fostered, don't you remember that litter of newborns and the month I didn't sleep for more than an hour a night?"

"Jackson, seriously, have you ever fostered?"

My bald head turned radiantly purple-red.

"Um . . . come to think of it, um, I guess, no, I have not."

"Well," said Stephanie brightly, "we'll take care of that, won't we, Jackson?"

"We . . . err . . . yes. We will. Yes," I said, smiling through my teeth, feeling a single forced-out bead of sweat fall in my eye.

I didn't want to foster. I had no time, I had no room in my life for another animal. My commitment was to my plan, my band, my music, the destiny I had to fight for. Paying attention to something else would ruin my mojo.

Or at least that's what I told myself—while my inner brat was busy stamping his feet, flinging snot and wailing, "Don't wanna! Don't wanna!" I was face-to-face with the very nature of my self-centeredness.

The barely concealed truth was that fostering an animal would destroy the ease with which I'd arranged my world. I was truly involved in my shelter work, but when I wasn't there, my to-do list for the day involved getting loaded, going to band rehearsal, having a nightcap or six, and going to sleep. I had no deep responsibility to anybody but myself. I had cats, sure, but they were already part of my routine—in other words, they were easy. Bringing a foster animal into my life, on the other hand, would have meant actually expending energy on a living thing, not just routine energy but focused energy, and that was the last thing I wanted. I felt like I was doing just plenty between the hours of nine and five. And now I was exposed as the narcissistic bullshitter that I was.

The problem with being a narcissistic bullshitter is that, when somebody calls you on your narcissistic bullshit in front of an audience, there's nowhere for you to run. The positive side of this, however, is that, when none of your hiding places are available, you have a unique opportunity to change. So when Stephanie picked me up and plopped me naked right in the middle of moral nowhere, despite the pesky but predictable cameo from the fear/doubt shotgun, loosed from its cabinet and staring at me, I decided to take advantage of the moment and declare myself ready for the challenge.

That challenge came a lot sooner than I thought it would.

The next day, during a staff meeting before opening, through the slats of the blinds that Cheeks had bent to match his tubby shape so he could watch birds and children from a safe distance, I saw someone jump out of her car with one of our cardboard cat carriers, walk hurriedly to the front door, drop the carrier, and jog back, looking nervously over her shoulder like she'd just left a flaming bag of shit on the porch and rung the doorbell. I ran to the door and caught her as she was getting back in the car.

"I can't keep him," she said. I opened my mouth to ask for information about the cat—any information at all—but this woman was obviously terrified that I was going to try to make her feel guilty (I wasn't) or ask for money (I was); her defense tactic was to speak as quickly as possible and not let me get a word in edgewise. "I adopted him a year ago when he was a kitten, his name is Omni, he was hit by a car yesterday and the vet says his pelvis is badly broken, I can't afford—"

"But—"

"—the bills, you know, I'm just a student, for chrissakes, and besides, he didn't like being outside much, and I want him to be an outdoor cat, you know, I think cats should be—"

"Why don't you—"

"—free to roam in the wild, don't you think, well, not in the wild, I mean, but I just don't think animals were meant to live indoors, and also we never really bonded, it's been a year, he doesn't—"

"Okay, we can—"

"—cuddle, he doesn't play, I don't think he likes me, and really? If you don't like me, then I don't like you, either, so I guess that's it." Then a pause that took us both off guard. "I don't like him."

Strike three, game over.

So an hour later, forms signed and the woman a thankfully distant memory, I'm driving the cat to our vet clinic across town, when at a stoplight I realize I have no idea what he looks like. I open up the top of the carrier. His head comes up slightly. He's obviously not going anywhere. His pain is written all over him, despite his feline stoicism. I notice a gray spot on his nose and it's so cute I can't help laughing. I sense Omni's suspicion immediately upon eye contact—cats, having a prey response heightened to a fine point, are practitioners of "trust but verify" diplomacy. I once heard a lifetime American ambassador being interviewed about negotiations with the Albanians after the fall of communism. They were so isolated for so many years, so independent of the West, that they had never needed to ask for inclusion in the world's sandbox; they were arrogant, surly, suspect. He was constantly fighting his previous knowledge of their abhorrent record on human rights. But he said that his mission as a diplomat was to establish a line in to a completely closed culture through the concept of empathy. Feel for the culture in a noncondescending but present way, feel for the life circumstances of the human sitting across the table from you, and then communication in the absence of linguistic and cultural familiarity can begin. Imagine yourself as the person across the table from you. This concept resonated deeply with me, and I had been using it as a character-building cornerstone. First and foremost, whether dealing with a feral or just a new arrival to the shelter, confused and disoriented, I am an ambassador. Later I will be your friend, but for now, I come from a world you don't know or trust, but I carry a friendly message.

I start with the slow blink, the Cat I Love You that allows him to perceive me without having to put up his guard. Imagine being the Albanian ambassador and I greet you with a respectful "*Tungjatjeta,*" in perfect southern Gheg dialect. Or how about that iconic scene in the film *Close En-*

counters of the Third Kind. Imagine being the aliens, being greeted by that now-familiar five-note cadence. You might not trust, but you would be hard-pressed not to say, "I'm listening. . . ."

At some point the cars honking behind me let me know the light had turned green, but as I drove on I was still lost with this cat. This boy obviously hadn't had much experience with faith, with having an advocate; I wanted to try to be that for him. I'd been playing around with some non-threatening scent-introduction techniques and presented him with the earpiece of my glasses. This was a rational second step; not familiar enough for flesh-pressing, I give you a gift of my culture—my scent from a distance, a gilded Statue of Liberty paperweight. He reacted positively again, cheek marking my scent on the glasses, handing me back a Rozafa Castle snow globe.

His diplomatic green light allowed permission for the final step: the actual handshake. Instinctually, I put my finger to what I thought of as the cat's third eye—between the eyes and an inch or two up; touch and wait for him to push my finger back to his ears, completing the cycle, going from touch to pet—and I swear it was the first time I felt a cat sigh. He didn't just sigh with his body, his mouth, and lungs. He sighed with his entire being, and I felt it. I'd used the slow blink, the eyeglasses, and the third-eye techniques separately, but it wasn't until this moment, wondering how to introduce myself as a nonthreatening ambassador, that I thought to combine them in a sort of three-step cat diplomacy handshake that gave me a piece of understanding I'd never had before. Game over the second time in one day; I had my foster care beta tester, and he had crystallized a new method: the three-step handshake.

That terrible name, though, had to go. I looked at him and thought, *Omni? Really? Who would name you Omni? Just so disconnected from you. I'm sorry you had to hang with an idiot.* He gave me a matter-of-fact gaze as if to say, *Let me tell you—not a picnic.* In that moment I realized he reminded me of an old friend, a brilliant composer who at most times seemed to regard the world with a mixture of bemusement and disgust. I pictured him scribbling a full symphony at my dining room table while listening to the Rolling Stones on his Walkman. In homage to Ben Weisser, I would rename this cat Benny. I began a daydream of life with Benny, the brilliant cat who I would teach to love "Exile on Main Street." I would give his new adopters a copy of the record. They would think me a perfect clown. I wouldn't care.

That serene dream of smooth sailing on the foster parent sea lasted an entire half hour.

"There's serious damage to his pelvis," said the vet, pointing at the X-rays she'd taken of Benny. "He'll most likely have nerve damage, and his left rear leg shows no

Meeting a New Cat? Try the Three-Step Handshake

1. Use the slow-blink Cat I Love You technique discussed in the previous chapter to break the language barrier.

2. Do you wear glasses? Take them off and present the cat with the tip of an earpiece. It's not as threatening as your hand, and it is heavy with scent from the area just behind the ears that's loaded with your signature smell. Let him sniff and hopefully rub a cheek on the earpiece. If you don't wear glasses, try putting a pen or pencil behind your ear for a bit and then offer it to him.

3. Take a finger, let him sniff it like he did the glasses or pen, and bring that finger toward the spot between and just above his eyes. Let him meet your finger with his head and push against it until you've made a fluid move from the bridge of his nose up to between the ears. It's a mutual gesture, like a handshake or an embrace. There: you're no longer strangers.

reflex response at all, which means we'll probably have to amputate."

"Um . . . okay," I said in an overly matter-of-fact way. I just wanted to deflect any discussion of euthanasia to save his pain and our mounting expense. I provided him a serene touch, just a little something to ground him in comfort among the exploring and colder touches of the vet staff. "So what do I . . . do?" Deep breath. Please let us *do* something that doesn't involve blue juice. . . .

"For now, just keep him in a big carrier in your apartment and give the pelvic bone time to heal. In six weeks bring him back and, barring an act of God, we'll remove the leg."

"No rehab?" I asked. "Nothing?"

"He needs to be pretty stationary. That is his rehab. He just needs to heal."

"No, but you don't understand, I'm Cat Boy, I have this whole plan, and—"

Doc Rachel smiled weakly. She was a great early advocate, teaching me much about the feline machine. She was used to my growing eccentricities. "That's great, Cat Boy. He needs to be stationary and he needs time to heal."

Some cat advocate I was turning out to be. Get a cat to trust me, keep him in a box for a month and a half, and then cut his leg off.

At least Benny's health issues meant that this would be a

pretty easy foster for my first case. If he was going to live in a carrier, I figured, that meant he'd be separated from the other cats in the house, which meant no messy introductions. And there would be just a bit of separation between me and him—enough to keep me from adopting him. Once again I had fallen victim to an idyllic daydream of my time with Benny—and we know where that leads (insert sound of face being slapped hard).

My roommate Kate, the drummer in my band and one of my closest friends, who knew me as an emerging cat-obsessive, was smarter than I and wary of our new arrival. We already had some social issues to contend with—namely my seventeen-pound hunk of holy-terror-inspiring dominance named Rabbi, who chased Kate's cats Samantha and Maggie so relentlessly that Kate finally had to build a fortress of couch cushions around her futon so that she could sleep without cat fights erupting in the middle of the night. Rabbi's physical and emotional inverse was my other cat, Velouria, who was six pounds on her heaviest day. The two of them were the manifestation of feline yin and yang; ultimate predator and prey. Where Rabbi was fight—big but deceptive in his demanding stealth and speed, the cat equivalent of a rhino—she was flight—the ultimate victim-in-waiting, blindingly quick with an insane vertical jump, all in a tiny frame. (I'd thought for weeks after adopting her that she was a few-months'-old Maine Coon kitten; she turned out to be three years old.) She was Rabbi's very favorite furry toy. She really, truly hated being Rabbi's favorite toy. So I understood why Kate was worried. Rabbi, Samantha, Maggie, and Velouria made a volatile enough mix without adding a completely unknown element.

The first month or so was surprisingly uneventful. Benny showed no interest in anybody or anything. In retrospect, I understand that his apathy was simply forcible adaptation to the size of his immediate surroundings. Plus, even with the copious medications flowing through his veins for that first few weeks, he was still in obvious discomfort standing, walking, and using his litter box. The other cats circled his carrier with regularity. It was like that movie *Warriors*, when the gang has to get from one end of New York to the other, coming across rival gangs along the way. All the other cats were taunting Benny: "Oh Warrior! Come out to play-ay!!"

Even when Benny was finally allowed to come out to play-ay, a month into his stay with us, his lingering physical issues made his first explorations tentative. But there was something else; a manner to him that I found curious and often kind of hilarious. He would walk into the living room, look around, and look at himself—literally take stock, his paws, his tail—and his bewilderment was palpable. It was as if Benny, bus driver and eternal bachelor, had hit his well-worn La-Z-Boy, tired from his ten-hour shift, eaten a Swanson's Hungry-Man and fallen asleep, fork in hand, only to wake up curled in a donut bed next to a dying fern, his nose in his own ass. He walks out to the living room, trying to shake off a bad dream he's already left behind, and freezes in realization: ". . . a cat? I'm a freaking *cat*?" The tail flicks of its own accord and he jumps. He tries, unsuccessfully, to navigate a world with four legs, paws, and claws. He takes a step, examines his new body. He looks around the room from a vantage point he's never experienced before. He wants to get to a mirror pronto to see what the hell is going on, but the only one is above the bathroom sink. With his left rear leg still obviously causing a problem, there was no way he was going to jump from the floor to the sink just so he could witness the horror. He dragged the leg behind him and would often whip back in midstride and gnaw at it like it was an unwelcome visitor, grooming it obsessively like if he could just give it a bath it wouldn't be so annoying. I can't count how many times we would turn our heads for a moment and turn them back to find that his leg had gotten stuck between the crisscrosses of bamboo of the Pier 1 rattan Papasan chair that was de rigueur for everybody on a budget those days. Benny would cry out and we would pull him out, cringing and thinking, "Ouch—legs aren't supposed to twist that way. . . ."

Obviously, the leg would be coming off. It wasn't a big deal; I knew plenty of "tripods" who had gotten along just fine in life. Kate, however, took a different view; from the

way she objected you'd think it was her own leg we were dis-
cussing. "Fine," I said to her. "Let's make a deal. We'll
schedule the surgery, but if you can rehab him before then
and he's not getting his leg caught in the chair or loops of
fabric from the carpet or invisible leg traps that we can't
see but that immobilize him, we'll call it off." The deal was
just a formality; Kate knew as much about rehabbing a cat's
leg as I knew about cutting it off. Besides, we still had no
idea whether there was nerve damage. I set the surgery for
a month from that day. And still, Kate doggedly pursued a
course of isometrics. She got him on his side and pushed his
leg gently up toward the pelvis, let it relax again, pushed,
relaxed, pushed, relaxed. She did this for weeks with almost no response from Benny. Unless his getting annoyed
enough to bite her counts as a response.

I delayed the surgery upon Kate's insistence. She could
be very insistent. Then, finally, six weeks later, the order
came down from the shelter gods that we had to either amputate the leg so we could move into the next phase of Benny's foster care, which would involve socialization and
readjustment to territory with his new physical challenges
(how would being a tripod affect his litter-box habits? how
would he handle linoleum?), or bring him back and put him
up for adoption.

Still, though, she wouldn't stop pushing that leg, letting

it relax, push, relax, push, relax. She did it over breakfast, she did it before rehearsal, and nothing was happening. It got to the point where I was starting to feel sorry for her. Until one night, as we were watching TV, something changed.

"Oh, shit, Jackson! Jackson! Jackson! Look at this!"

I didn't look. "Cool." I was busy being annoyed that her new haircut was blocking my view of the TV.

"No, look!"

"I am."

"Get *over* here." She dragged me off the couch by the sheer force of her stink eye, waited for me to settle, and pushed his leg up toward his pelvis—and he resisted.

I was shocked out of my stupor. "Holy shit," I said. "Do that again." She did. More resistance. "Let me try!" She did. Then he bit me. I definitely had that coming.

I remembered what Doc Rachel had said about "no reflex response" and "nerve damage." *Good job, buddy*, I thought, surprised that I suddenly cared about keeping the leg. *Way to show her!*

As the days went by, Benny started offering more resistance, pushing more and more against Kate's hand. Once I realized that there was a chance the leg might be saved, I joined in the rehab enthusiastically, even though it did involve admitting I was wrong.

Pushing back on a hand, though, was one thing; actually using the leg was another, and the clock was ticking.

Benny was scheduled for surgery on Wednesday morning. Literally at the eleventh hour, during his last-chance Tuesday late-night rehab session, it was as if he was suddenly made aware that his leg was going to be cut off. "Excuse me? You actually *meant* that??!" He leapt up and began running around the house, over shelves, across tables, under beds. "Seriously!! Let's be rational here! Look . . . look. Look here, goddammit! It works! I'll wiggle my toes! Chase bugs! Climb the shelves! Papasan chair, take *that*! Hey, human, are you freaking watching me? Here—I'll run up to you, bite your ankle, and escape like I'm made of fog! Cut my leg off? I don't *think* so, you . . . you . . . fucker—I thought we had an understanding!!"

This did nothing for the I-fell-asleep-in-a-chair-and-now-I'm-a-*what?* expression; all it meant was that he was bewildered, but moving faster. It was midnight. I was going to have to call Doc Rachel in the early morning and cancel the appointment again. In fact, now I was going to have to beg for the leg. Not for another extension, but to explain the act of god she had half-jokingly referred to two months earlier. In this moment of watching Benny's triumph over fate, I felt something shift and realized that, whether he ended up a tripod or not, it was game over once again.

Cat Daddy

Benny wasn't my foster cat anymore. He was my family.

Kate disagreed violently, and that honestly shocked the hell out of me. Having rehabbed him, she was happy to return him to the shelter to be adopted by the right family. Now I was going to have to bargain with Doc Rachel to keep his leg and with Kate to keep the rest of him. What Kate was willfully ignoring was that *I* was the right family. When you go to the shelter to adopt a pet, we told our visitors, you have to try not to feel overwhelmed by the numbers, by that feeling of "I just want to take them all home." You don't pick an animal; an animal will pick you. So it was with Benny—watching him run around the apartment to keep us from amputating his leg, I realized he'd picked me. The teacher arrived when the student was ready to learn. Through a combination of begging, bargaining, cajoling, pleading, manipulation, and lies—virtually every con I had ever picked up—I managed to convince Kate to let Benny stay. He gradually—*very* gradually—started to get used to his new home, and it seemed like things were finally settling down for him, at least a little. He'd had so much tumult in his short life; it must have been heaven to be in a place where things stayed the same.

That didn't last long; the concept of "same" in my life was a barely contained inside joke. Our lease ran out and we decided that rather than pay the increased rent, we would use our money to record a proper album. Money that we would generate by magically finding a place where the whole band could live and rehearse and where the cops would come over only every other night. In the meantime we had to go—winding up in the welcoming arms of Kate's boyfriend Jeremy's house.

It was a Victorian, and like most houses from that period, big and confining at the same frustrating time—I guess Victorians liked living in places where there wasn't room enough for them to actually move. Jeremy and Kate slept in the master, Jeremy had another friend staying in another bedroom, Beth, my band's keyboardist, was in another, and I was in the fourth, which was more like a Victorian closet. In addition to our five cats (Rabbi, Benny, Velouria, Samantha, and Maggie), Jeremy already had a cat, Trapper, his friend had a dog, and there was also a very loud bird that nobody would admit to owning.

At first there were no problems; the animals, four- and two-legged alike, went about our business as if nothing were amiss. Rabbi was the benevolent corrections officer, making his rounds and keeping peace among the inmates, all of whom—including Benny—respected his rule. By this time Rabbi and his rhinotude had already struck so much fear into Velouria, Samantha, and Maggie that they gave way to him simply because it was the easiest thing to do. Benny, for his part, remained a detached observer.

But not for long.

One night the five of us humans settled on Jere's couch, staring at the TV. Benny was parked underneath the TV stand, staring at us staring at the TV. As Rabbi walked by, he crossed paths with Benny. This kind of path-crossing usually has the same look; if two cats are on the same stretch of track, neither ceding right of way to the other, they'll sniff one another and glare until somebody blinks or hisses or raises a paw, breaking the tension and ending the game of chicken. Benny showed no out-of-the-ordinary body language at all.

Then he struck like a snake.

Where one moment there were two calm cats exchanging information through their gaits, their eyes, their tails, in the next a mass of fur rolls around the floor like a robot vacuum cleaner gone berserk, scratching, screaming louder than a kindergarten class in a haunted house—

—and then perfectly still for an instant, somehow two cats again—just long enough to think, *maybe I can reach over and grab—*

—and then it explodes again, like the plunger pulled on a pinball machine, and an all-devouring ball of feline anger launches toward the front of the house, hits the front door, bounces off and retraces its gruesome tracks toward the back, and then rolling faster and scratching harder and screaming louder, and faster and harder and louder, hitting the back door, ravaging again toward the front, moving in a manner that was funny and horrifying at the same time down the hallway, and just as I think that this is the longest catfight I have ever seen, there comes another instant where they are two cats again, and in that instant Rabbi does something he's never done before: he turns tail and runs.

 Defuse the Cat Bomb!

After living with people for any length of time, cats and other animals will adapt their behavior to mirror that of the humans around them. Issues of aggression often display themselves during energetic spikes: the "waking up and getting ready for work/ school" spike, the "coming home and getting ready for dinner" spike, and the "closing up shop and getting ready for bed" spike.

Knowing your spikes means you can head off potential moments of overstimulation for your cats. If you engage your cats in play ten minutes before a spike, redirecting their energy in an appropriate way, you can defuse the cat bomb.

I go instantly into fierce, overprotective mother mode. "No, Benny, bad cat, Rabbi, Rabbi, where are you, oh,

God, wait, are you under that table, is that blood?? Shit, no, Benny, how could you, oh, God, Rabbi, yes, come to me, come on, come on, you don't need to hide all the way behind the couch, Kate, get behind the couch, Jere, what are you doing sitting there—help me goddammit! Come on, come on, COME ON, Kate, get out of my way, help me move the couch, okay, Rabbi, here I am, Jere, will you grab Benny? Gently—just put him in the bathroom—turn off the lights. Oh, Rabbi, thank God, it's all right, I'll make everything okay, are you hurt, oh, sorry, I don't mean to squeeze you so hard, Benny, you fuck!, Rabbi, please forgive me, Benny what kind of . . . you little fucking monster! Oh, God, Rabbi, please be okay."

When Rabbi had first shown up at my door (literally, I opened the door and looked down at a four-week-old kitten), not knowing any better, I set him in the living room in the middle of four other cats (rather than giving him a safe "base camp" in which to decompress and learn the scent of the territory). Completely panicked, he scampered up to a windowsill, where he stayed for the next four hours, sitting perfectly erect, taking in the subtle movements of every two-legged and four-legged beast around him. He did this until his tiny little kitten body could take no more, at which point he went to sleep, fell off the windowsill, and face planted on the living room carpet.

Seven years, two states, and eight homes later, I'd never

seen him scared again. He was Big Daddy, close to nineteen pounds and the protector of all things predictable, the champion of stability—which is necessary for cat coexistence, especially in larger communities.

New Cat Arrival? Set up Base Camp!

Whoever says that when introducing cats to one another you should "just let 'em sort it out" is dead wrong. When introducing cats to cats:

- Set up base camp. New arrivals need to feel secure in their territory. Start them in a space small enough to claim, with their own belongings and equal doses of your own scent and theirs.
- Introduce via positive associations. Mealtime is your perfect opportunity—introduce cats to one another through scent *only*, by feeding them on opposite sides of a closed door. Work in cat-to-cat eye contact during mealtime at *their* pace, not yours!
- Practice site swapping. Make it clear that

no one cat, or one group, owns the home.
Everyone owns everything, just at different
times of the day.

• Know when to say when. Use your intuition to
know when to try letting everyone out together. Setbacks are inevitable, but chaos is
preventable.

But the stable social structure had come gracelessly tumbling down before my eyes. And my response was the an-
tithesis of what I preach today. Now I'm all about showing
my clients (and anyone else who will listen) the value of becoming semidetached observers. Watch what's happening so
that you can report back to me in detail, and I can string the
moments together in a way so that cat sense makes human
sense. It's the emotional entanglement that gets human and
cat nowhere (and naturally continues the negative dynamic
between the animals).

The timing couldn't have been worse; we were about to
play our first gig at the Fox Theater, the biggest venue in the
valley. Three days later, when the gig was over, I took Rabbi
to see Doc Rachel. He hadn't sustained any real injuries
during the fight—his nose was scratched and a few tufts of
hair were missing, but that's to be expected when two cats

get in a brawl—but he had lost his swagger, his cat mojo. He was navigating the house like a pariah, tiptoeing around the edges. I told her that there just had to be a reason for what amounted to an abdication of the throne. All I could think of was this documentary I'd seen on lion prides in the Serengeti. At some point the alpha cat of the pride grew fat and old, was challenged, and, humiliatingly (from my perspective, at any rate), was run off by a young-buck challenger.

But Rabbi was only seven. Fat? Yeah. But not old.

"Well, it looks like Rabbi and Benny understood what was going on a lot better than their humans did," said Doc Rachel. "Rabbi's diabetic."

"That's bullshit," I said. "He . . . he's not drinking excessively, he's not losing weight, his appetite hasn't changed, Christ, he's grooming regularly—he doesn't even have dandruff."

"Look," She handed me the analysis, and of course she was right. "He has the glucose levels of a pot of honey."

The situation I couldn't understand then is clear to me now as I write this: The makeup of the cat society had changed, and Rabbi, with his health problem, was sending out signals that he was no longer the best cat to keep stability in the daily time-sharing rituals. The group had grown larger and more complex, and at the same time his ability to keep it stable and safe had diminished, especially in the face of this incredibly high-stress time of territorial instability and transition. It was amazing to watch what happened over the next few weeks. Rabbi was *relieved*. His body became more relaxed, he was now content to lie down and observe rather than skulking unhappily on the fringes of the community. Rather than face the stress and pressure of performing a task he wasn't up to, he was glad to step down and let Benny do the job he could no longer do himself.

Rabbi, sadly, slid downhill head-spinningly fast. He was resistant to every treatment we tried: sheep insulin, human insulin, you name it. He quickly developed the symptoms I'd told the vet were absent—an insatiable thirst which meant he urinated constantly, peripheral neuropathy (weakness in and eventually lack of control of his rear legs, which made litter-box trips a nightmare), and precipitous weight loss. (Little did I know at the time that I had a choice: instead of insulin, I could have switched him to a grain-free meat diet alone, and it might have saved his life. Once I learned this, years later, I blamed Doc Rachel for a while for not being educated in cat nutrition—but just like I couldn't play victim to the doctors who prescribed me narcotics for so many years, I have to accept my own responsibility for not educating myself.)

Rabbi left us about four months later, and Benny, Ve-

The Catkins Diet

Cats are carnivores, born to hunt prey and eat it. Not wheat, corn, or even fish. Meat. A high-protein, low-carb diet is what's best for the long-term health of felines.

I prefer a raw diet for cats—yes, raw meat, especially since it's become so easy to prepare, thanks to small companies dedicated to providing animals high-quality meaty alternatives. Being obligate carnivores, cats have a short, straight digestive tract perfectly suited for eating raw meat. Besides, you never see a cat in a field roasting a mouse over a spit, right? That being said, if a raw diet is too much, just stick to the "Catkins Diet" and seek out a high-quality grain-free wet food. How do you know high-quality? The same as you know for you; read the ingredients!

I know there are some out there who say, "Pshaw—I've always fed my cats the same kibble and my last cat died at twenty-three." I'm sure you've seen stories of 112-year-old humans who attribute their longevity to a steady diet of absinthe and Cuban cigars. Sure, it happens—but why bank on luck?

louria, and I moved into a new place with Beth, who had just broken up with her girlfriend. My history with her was as long as my tenure in Boulder, and its dynamic had become pretty predictable: we played music and got each other high. We were enablers of the highest order. We invited few people over, and the only place we ever spent time besides rehearsal and work was at our dealer's house.

Over the next few years my using went from bad to ridiculous. Whatever remaining shreds of pretense I had held on to disappeared; when I think of that apartment, all I can see is the garden-level quicksand pit where I became exactly what I had always feared. I couldn't tell people I was "partying" anymore, so I just didn't tell them anything. I hid in my bedroom, gradually even away from Beth. I was even too ashamed to use in front of my using buddy because she never did anything besides smoke weed and occasionally drink whiskey while she played pool. I was alone in my room, chopping coke, making lines, remaking them, reveling in the perfection of the ritual. Quiet, small movements.

I'm not getting high to go anywhere. I'm going through beautiful motions. Under my own spell. The coke snort is, by its nature, loud but carefully disguised by rustling paper just in case Beth can hear. Clean it up with a finger to the small mirror and a freeze rub to the gums. Now I'm jacked enough to start the rest of our program; first we take a handful of Klonopin. We have forty minutes till blast-off. That's fifteen minutes to polish off what's left of the wine, go out to the living room to share my weed from one of our many bongs, pipes, etc. Since weed stinks (especially the increasingly fine shit we were buying), I can't hide that in my room—have to share. Then, after getting high, sneak back into my room to "pee" (a few more lines to stave off passing out)—I come out "nursing" a fine glass of Australian Shiraz (that's right, I actually thought I was a connoisseur, not an alcoholic). And THEN I pass out. To this day, I don't know whether Beth understood, the few times she discovered me facedown in the kitchen, that I had ODed. It happened, to my memory (admittedly spotty), three times. It was too dark for her to see that I was facedown in spit and little bits of puked-up wine. She asked "Hey, you OK?" and as I struggled to say "No—I can't get up, please get me in bed. I can't crawl. My arms are too jelly. I can't even get to my knees. I'm too big, I know, but you can just drag me and I'll get into bed? Just don't panic and take me to the hospital." But nothing would come out. And she would go back to bed. Our relationship, begun when she was underage and I was some kind of driven songwriting savant, continued through years of struggle and ridiculous gigs in the middle of Colorado winter, wrecking our van on a freeway and still making it for the set, sharing proper beds (she was such a hardcore lesbian even *I* didn't try to seduce her), backseats of cars, running out of gas in the middle of the desert and laughing about it—our relationship had come to this. Lying ridiculously half alive in the kitchen and her leaving me there. This is your friendship; this is your friendship on drugs. Any questions?

My work at the shelter was consumed, unsurprisingly, by the same quicksand. When the capital campaign for a new building went into full swing, I would go into strategy meetings first thing in the morning. Fifteen minutes and a quad latte later, I'd excuse myself to go into the bathroom, sit on the toilet, and fall asleep. As outreach director, I was responsible for making the word of the Humane Society good in the public eye and showing people how we were a vital part of the community, and I was good at this—but I was used to doing it in classrooms, at pet stores, not in the paper, over the radio, not on any larger scale. I had become very skilled at improvising my presentations while pharmaceutically quicksanded, but what was called for here was far beyond my capabilities. So, naturally, I was shocked when they replaced me as outreach director.

. . .

It would've been really easy for them to fire me. I wasn't getting the job done. Instead, they recognized my value. I think what I was doing with cats outweighed my incompetence as an administrator. The alternative they gave me was to keep doing my cat work and head up the mobile pet adoption unit (PAU), which was me (a dangerously broke-down Cat Daddy), driving around in a (dangerously broke-down) Winnebago full of animals and one volunteer, three or four times a week.

This was a welcome change. I was really good at it, and out from the confines of the building, out in the world, not just bringing the concept of animal stewardship to the community, but actually bringing the animals to the people was so breathably simple and direct. Every day I'd make my rounds with my volunteer; we'd pick five or six cats and one dog (and sometimes a rabbit) to go out with us for the day to a supermarket, a street fair, a festival—you name it. I'd always pick the animals that needed the exposure the most, meaning they'd been at the shelter for a long time, showed signs of going a little kennel-crazy, or were "too" something: too old, too fat, too timid, too bold, too black to easily go into a home. The staff would tell me, "Hey, listen, this guy needs to get out of here," and I'd pick him up and off we'd go.

"Mommy, mommy, come look at the kitties!" I would hear

as I sat at the diner-type booth inside the PAU in the parking lot of a supermarket, highlighting passages in the behavior book I'd read through once already that morning.

"Okay, Joey, after we have lunch and Mommy has convinced the store to take back the machine they sold her that does everything but what they said it would do . . ." the answer would come. Twenty minutes later a poor, beleaguered woman with a hyperactive six-year-old would be standing in front of me, and I'd put down the flash cards I'd made while they were in the store, and I'd introduce the kid to the cat in a way that allowed the mother a few moments' peace. Sometimes, half an hour later, as my volunteer quizzed me, Joey's mom would have realized that a cat was just what they needed, and as they drove away, I'd know that yet another cat was on its way to a good home. On days when we had fewer visitors, I'd work out a new technique in my head and turn to the cat or the dog (or sometimes the rabbit) and see if what I was thinking held water. I was incredibly lucky to have a job that gave me such an opportunity for learning about behavior. In the end, the PAU found homes for so many cats that we qualified for a grant, to help pay for me to design and have built a brand-new adoption cruiser.

In the meantime, the live rock scene in Boulder had been dying on the vine. Other friends' bands that we had played so many shows with were scattering like roaches to Chicago, Austin, Seattle. We should have known when the Fox Theater, the most kickass place in the area to play, started a night called Disco Inferno, with a DJ. It immediately did so well that the ripple effect started spreading to other clubs, and the bands froze as if we had been hit with a collective bat, just like the hair metal bands on the Sunset Strip dove for cover when Nirvana hit big. Pope of the Circus Gods started having trouble, both financial and interpersonal—we fought all the time—and finally, a year or two after I took over the PAU, the band broke up.

Through all this, however, I was still working hard in the world of cats, where I was affectionately known by this point as "Cat Boy." I wrote articles for our newsletter and for newsletters of other shelters ("Cat Mojo 101"; "Cat Boy's Holiday Dos and Don'ts"), I was starting to give workshops to the staff at our shelter and to other shelter workers, volunteers, foster parents, and so on. Then Danielle, our CEO, had what I consider to be a game-changing idea; she started pushing me toward the concept of at-home consults for behavior. She thought it was worth the shelter's dime (and the possibly empty cage) to send me out when somebody would call and say, "I'm about to bring my cat in to you guys, I can't take this anymore."

"What's going on?" I would say when I got to the house.

"My cat won't stop peeing on my kids' toys," the harried mother would say. "They're all under the age of eight and he's ten, and I think he resents them. I don't want to make a choice between my kids and my cat, but I—"

"Don't go there yet, OK? Come over here. Let's look at this litter box."

"Okay."

"Now look at the toys."

"Okay."

"See how the toys are forming a fortress around the litter box? Making loud noises and moving on their own? He probably feels surrounded and attacked by chaotic energy."

"Really? He's not saying he hates my kids?"

"No. He's saying, *I HATE this feeling! I own this space, and it is under attack!* Your cat is defending the Alamo. All you need to do is create a different play area for your kids or a different Alamo area for your cat. If he doesn't have to share, he won't feel threatened, and it'll stop."

"It can't be that simple."

"It's not simple or not simple. It's trying on a different pair of glasses, you know?"

But it was simple; it was a pretty basic problem, a sympathetic solution and one more cat who didn't have to come to the shelter. These at-home visits were gold for my new process. It was essential that these guardians understand cat mojo, or how cats see the world.

This was the outcome of about seventy-five percent of my

house calls. The other twenty-five percent of the time, the guardians in question really just wanted permission to surrender. I would fix the leak and they would get the Look on their faces (Benny's former guardian had had the Look), a panicked expression even they probably hadn't expected, and suddenly another leak would spring. I would stop the cat from peeing on the wall and suddenly it was, "I think my son is allergic to the cat." Or, "You know, we were thinking of having a baby anyway and I heard that they aren't good with babies." Once it became clear what was going on, I began a form of shelter triage, trying my best to reason with the guardians until I was sure beyond a shadow of a doubt that re-homing was the best (and ultimately only) option.

The other consults I would do were for cats who had just been adopted from the shelter, to help keep them in the homes they'd just gone to. This sounds elementary, but it was a step instituted by Danielle because it led to a reduction in pet returns. Every four-legged body that didn't come back to the shelter was an animal that didn't have that black mark of being returned for litter-box issues or being bad with kids or other pets, a black mark that could lead her to being euthanized for lack of space either at our shelter or another one.

Millions were raised and a state-of-the-art shelter built, but, selfishly, I found it a mixed blessing. On the one hand, it was new. Spanking, gleaming, spaciously, hygienically new. Solitary caging for cats who didn't play well with others, group living condos for those who did, better soundproofing, a central meet-and-greet room—wonderful improvements, especially if you're a cat.

But there was also a distinct separation between the administrative world and the animal world. Even though the old building had had two stories, offices were strewn throughout both of them, wherever there was space; with all of the positions I'd held over the years, in fact, I never worked upstairs until we moved. In the new building, you could go upstairs to the administrative side and forget that there were any animals there. It didn't smell. There's something to be said about the smell of animal permeating every square inch of the building. You remember where you work. Some days I just wouldn't remember unless I was out with the adoption unit, or I would just force myself to go downstairs and work with the cats. It just didn't feel like our building anymore. It's probably bullshit on my part to romanticize the nights where we would run around with buckets to stop the rain from flooding the old place because the ceiling was full of holes, but those kinds of experiences have the ability to galvanize people. It's like when you're young and you passionately love a shabby band that only you and your friends know about—until they sign with a major label, and then you and your buddies all disown them.

We had been a community. The move made us feel like a

corporation. I was mourning the loss and feeling lost myself. I've always been a little conflicted when it comes to my life getting big. I wish for *big*—big success, big acclaim, the biggest stage for big causes and big actions—but when *big* comes knocking it turns out to be the big, bad wolf, with sharp teeth, the better to eat me with. I was acutely aware that my time at the shelter was drawing to a close. I was also getting hints from the universe and friends (not necessarily in that order) that I *could* move on and become an independent contractor. The only other cat behaviorist I knew told me one day that she wanted to close up shop and that, any time I was ready, she would gladly refer her current and any future clients to me. I was already making decent money on my own time, doing at-home consults.

Then I met Jen.

Stuff That Broke and the Big Goddammit

The first time I laid eyes on Jen, I was working in the glass-enclosed showcase in the shelter lobby with a few of my more reticent, hard-to-place cat charges, frustrated because none of the slight adjustments I was making to hiding spots seemed to affect their confidence level. I was actually in the midst of hanging butcher paper on the glass. Maybe if we gave them the privacy they needed, I was thinking, and then gently desensitized . . . challenged them at their own pace. . . . Through the stripes of paper and outside world I saw a woman come in the front door, briefly address someone at the front desk, and start making her way toward the adoption area.

God, she's beautiful, I thought. *No,* I corrected myself, *she's hot.* It had been over a year since I had broken up with my last crazy girlfriend, and I was spiraling downward quickly enough that I knew I had to enter the social world again before my mojo completely left me. I caught up with her as she was walking out of the adoption area.

"Can I interest you in taking home one of my friends?" (This is why I don't do pickup lines.)

"I'm not ready. My cat died, and I'm just here to be around cat energy."

I switched immediately into grief counselor mode. Somehow I feel comfortable letting down my shield when it comes to opening up about the canyons of hurt our animals leave in us when they go. Helping people navigate their way through those canyons has always been a strange sort of honor.

She had inadvertently started a fire in her apartment complex, she told me, with one of the myriad candles she had burning around her home. As her complex was turning into an orange-and-red beast around her, she found one of her two cats plastered to the wall under her king-size bed; the bed was just way too heavy for her to move, and her cat was out of reach. Finally, to save herself and her other cat, she was forced to run out of the burning building.

Holy shit, my inner monologue continued. *This is tragic, Galaxy—tragic. Turn off the mojo, quick, for the love of God— before she catches you looking in her eyes, at her hair, or down her shirt!*

Self, I thought in response, *shut up. She's gorgeous. AND damaged. Which kind of makes her even hotter. Oh GOD. I just thought that. I need to get back into therapy for real.*

I don't ask women out. The best I can do when I see one in a restaurant or bar is turn my eyes all smoky and seductive, hoping it is construed as an invitation, or at least piques their imagination. And then I hope that they are so confident and liberated that they will take the "invite" and run with it. And that doesn't ever happen. When I see other guys try tired lines and not take no for an answer, finally walking away waving a napkin with her phone number on it like they've captured the flag, I always look on in disbelief, always wonder if I'm resentful or honest when I shake my head, saying under my breath, "If that's what game looks like, I'll sit this one out."

Luckily, I've been a performer most of my life. Between music and the theater, falling in love with someone has always been a natural occurrence. And as if by magic, the words "Do you want to go get some coffee?" came out of my mouth. I'm sure Jen shared my feelings of equal parts grief, attraction, and shame from acting on that attraction. Finding out today would require speaking to her, and getting that restraining order was hard enough in the first place. I'd just rather not risk it.

It was in October that we met, so on Halloween, I went over to Jen's apartment, where the two of us waited and waited and waited for her friend, dressed as if she was actu-

105

ally late to a Renaissance fair party next door, to realize that she was being ignored and leave. The moment that door shut with the two of us alone, I was literally thrown against it. I turned Jen around and grabbed her by the shoulders. This was not going to be a gentle affair. The next few hours were an explosive horn blast that signaled the beginning of an affair that made the eruption of Krakatoa look like a spilled glass of juice.

I speak from experience when I say, if you don't listen to that little voice in your head, and you ignore your friends when they say your new girlfriend is "edgy and not in a good way," you should at the very least listen to your animals. I didn't. But Benny and Velouria didn't like Jen at all. An avowed cat person, she would constantly grab them and squeeze. Eventually, whenever she reached for them I automatically winced in that oh-God-the-bomb's-about-to-go-off kind of way.

"It's great how much they love me!" she'd say after Velouria leapt out of her arms as if she'd been electrocuted. "Give mama a kiss," she'd say as she aimed her menacing head at Benny, and in the moment, I swear to God, I thought he looked like nothing more than Penelope Pussycat squirming wildly to avoid the loathsome embrace of Pepe Le Pew. When he escaped, he stood just off in the distance, looking at me in that way that reminded me again of Ben Weisser, the half-bemused, half-disgusted composer.

If my friend could have been with us, wearing a burgundy silk scarf and holding a long cigarette in a distinctively European way, he would have shaken his head and said, "Now *this* is going to be entertaining."

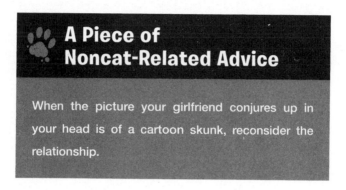

A Piece of Noncat-Related Advice

When the picture your girlfriend conjures up in your head is of a cartoon skunk, reconsider the relationship.

As Jen and I continued dating, Benny began making his displeasure clearer. His biting, for instance, always started cute. "Aww, he's just mouthy," I would say in my crazy cat-lady voice. But cute would escalate very quickly and often draw blood (not cute). He would get overstimulated, his body would simply take over, and then, to deal with his physical frustration, he would bite. This would happen even with people he knew and loved, so imagine how much worse it was with Jen, whom he detested.

One night Jen came over and Benny totally picked up on the fact that we had just had a huge fight. The first sign I had that the situation was dangerous came when we were sitting on the couch and Benny assumed a post on the couch cushion above our heads, which is, I was learning specifically from him, not a safe thing to let happen with cats who like to dominate space. He was in a classically offensive position, stalking from the other side of the couch with head low and rump high. And Jen looked over to him and they got locked in a momentary stare down. I saw what was coming, but before I could stop it, Jen tried to break the ice. "What's up, Bubba?" she started to say at the same time as I tried to say "whoa, whoa, WHOA!" but before either of us could even finish our respective three words, Benny slapped her across the head three times, knocking her glasses off her face, and then he went for a bite on her head. Whapwhapwhapchomp! All in the span of a second. Jen was deeply hurt—not physically, though I'm sure it was painful (you really feel those tooth bruises to bone for a while)—but more shocked that Benny would see her as a threatening trespasser, that he didn't love her back. This was a destructive dynamic that I had begun to observe more and more often in my clients and one I went to great pains to point out before their own projections brought their relationship irrevocably tumbling down. This wasn't about Jen; it was about the tension in the room, pushing Benny to that point of violent frustration.

Cat Projection 101

Step Away from the Cat's Brain!

When you are frustrated, you have picked the absolute *worst* time to decide you know what your cat is thinking. *Projection* is a defense mechanism in which we ascribe unwanted feelings onto others; so in this case, the angrier you get with your cat, the more apt you are to blame him, to say that he's acting out because he hates you.

Disengage and Observe

Instead of creating and living inside interspecies drama, see misbehavior as an opportunity to document patterns. So write them down, including as many details as possible. The more information you have, the easier it will be to figure out what's going on as you review even a week's worth of these patterns.

Afterward, given a bit of emotional space to process what I had seen, I knew one thing: I had to learn to sense when Benny was getting overstimulated, and once I knew what filled the balloon, I had to let the air out of it before it burst.

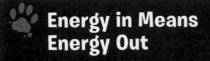

Energy in Means Energy Out

There's no reasoning with an overstimulated cat—you can't talk him down. You can, however, exercise him down, redirecting his energy onto an appropriate target like an interactive toy or even a laser pointer.

Here are some possible sources of overstimulation you might want to keep an eye out for:

- Petting-induced overstimulation
- Play aggression
- Environmentally induced overstimulation
- Energetic overstimulation

I had to train both him and myself. He was teaching me the deeper nature of himself and I owed it to him to do the thing that came hardest to me—listen. I had to also completely redefine the nature of overstimulation; it wasn't just a petting-induced by-product of the full-body over-stroke, what you would traditionally think of as "ramping him up"; the space itself could cause it—the people in my apartment, the rain on the roof, or just one person whose energy was completely sideways (more often than not). The territory was speaking ill; it rankled his skin and what was underneath just as much as if someone had screamed in his face or slapped him. As I tuned in to his sensitivity more and more in an effort to curb the violent quakes and aftershocks, I realized that he was already telling me about his frustration well before he bared his teeth, and I just hadn't been listening. Benny's meow was only uttered in times of disgust or frustration. It was decidedly one syllable and hoarse, the kind of hoarse that came from lack of use. Imagine the vague blend of being pissed off and startled you feel as you clear your voice and answer the phone at 4:00 a.m. That would be the sound, in cat. He would either vocalize, open his mouth slowly, or a combination of both, and then I knew it was about to be game on. When I saw his mouth just *start* opening, I would correct him—"Unh-unh!"—and his mouth would close and I'd praise him. No more would I give the cute mouthiness leeway, lest I also give passage to the beast underneath. Approaching a hand or a person in general with an open mouth was not an option. It took a long time and painstaking consistency. But it got done.

Say What?

Cats have over a hundred different kinds of vocalizations. Here are some of them:

Meowing is one of the rare times cats meet us halfway: Once they've reached adulthood, they only use meowing for us, not for each other. Just as we do the slow-blink Cat I Love You as a way to reach out to them, they meow as a way to reach out to us.

Purring is often a sign of happiness, but cats can also purr when ill or in distress. The remarkable purr is a vibration of the voice box that occurs at a frequency between 25 and 150 Hz, a frequency that is believed to promote healing and bone growth.

If you hear a cat *growling* or *hissing*, she's probably feeling threatened by something she needs to defend herself against.

If you've ever heard your cat make a *chirping* sound while watching birds, she's hypnotizing her prey!

Cat Daddy

. . .

Benny didn't outright kill Jen, though, so he must have been aware that there was something she could bring into my life. About a week after we met, I was on her balcony getting a buzz on from my friends, Mr. Flask and Ms. One-Hitter. When I stepped back in, she was waiting for me, standing a step back from the sliding glass door. "Listen," she said, "I'm a recovering drug addict and alcoholic."

Fuck, I thought. *Here it comes. . . .*

"I have over fifteen years clean and sober. If this goes anywhere, all I ask is two things. First, I don't really care what you do, but don't do it around me."

Well, that works, I continued my inner dialogue.

"Second, come to a meeting with me, just so you can see how I live." I think my inner dialogue went external for just a second. I might have sighed and looked skyward. I should've seen the setup from a mile away, but I didn't; I just thought that if I didn't go she'd stop having sex with me. And we couldn't let that happen.

There were hundreds of people at the Friday meeting, enough to make me feel comfortable going with Jen and disappearing into the crowd, especially because yes, I was very high. Jen had told me it was a speaker meeting, which also was a source of great relief since nobody would get mad at me if I didn't stand up and say, "Hi, my name is Jackson, and I am *so* not an addict/alcoholic." I was free to listen to these automatons, these Stepford Wives, swear on the burning bush that their lives were saved by faith in God and now they were free of the compulsion to get loaded, or whatever they would spew to make them feel better about themselves. Then I could go home with Jen, having done my boyfriendly duty, and get laid with the kind of wanton, furniture-throwing passion reserved for Hollywood summer blockbusters.

The speaker for the evening was Dmitri, a fast-talking lawyer in a business suit that would've paid my rent for three months. And even though he probably had been in that suit for fourteen hours, eaten two meals, gone to the gym, and been in court, he still made messy look damn good. He took a deep breath. Drink of water, elbows on the dais, smiled and heaved an out breath with the subtext, "long damned week? Who's with me?" Straightened back up again. Straightened his hopelessly unstraightenable tie. Finally: "Hey, I'm Dmitri and I'm an addict and an alcoholic." He said this with pride, almost like the spotlight was shining down on the Grand Ole Opry stage and he was saying, "Hello, I'm Johnny Cash." At that moment I released judgment for a second—Johnny Cash was an addict. In fact, Johnny, Ray Charles, Miles Davis, Stevie Ray Vaughan, Clapton . . . for every romantically tragic puke-choking victim, there was a survival story. And not just survival. These were artists who continued to make great art even after they'd abandoned the liquid muse. And this went through my head in an instant, between his intro and the fidgety first words of his story. I should've known in that instant that it was going to be a long night.

Dmitri talked for a solid hour, but it only took me five minutes to recognize myself in his film noir treatment of a "regular" life. "When my wife served me with divorce papers two days before Christmas, I mean whatever it shouldn't have bothered me, I'm Jewish, but in my state any way to shake my fist at God, any way to find a storm to rail against was good by me. Served by the same goddamned process-server punk that I used in my practice!" He laughed riotously, a cue for the sober hundreds to erupt with him. "I knew I needed to sign them but I couldn't, wouldn't, it was the last stand of my famous will, on Christmas Day 8:00 the kids were with her somewhere, she wouldn't even fucking tell me where they were, those poor kids, I imagined, Christmas in a Best Western somewhere without their Daddy because that bitch HAD to stand on ceremony, mind you I'm so shitfaced that I'm actually elaborating this out loud while drinking Courvoisier from the bottle, pausing to curse MY BAD LUCK as I burn my fucking lips on the pipe." There was no air in the room. Hundreds of people who knew this story by heart—it was their story—and yet, sympathizing with the protagonist of this movie as if his pain, his hubris, his blind headlong swan dive into the abyss, were unique. "She called, in one last act of mercy she wanted the boys to say Merry Christmas to Daddy who was 'on a business trip,' I'm not sure if I was just gone, whether it was the burns swelling my lips so I sounded like I was slurring more than I was, I don't know, she said in a way that cut through all of it, real calm, "I don't ever want to hear from you again. Ever, Dmitri. Can you even understand that?"

I surprise myself by tearing up. It's not like I hear his story and follow the trail of lightbulbs in my head to a sign in the sky saying, "I'm an addict and I accept a higher power in my life to restore me to sanity!" On the contrary: I begin squirming like I'm trying to get out of a straitjacket. I turn to Jen and blame those goddamn chairs, but the truth is laughably obvious. His life is totally different from mine, he has completely different problems, I don't use like him and he doesn't use like me, and I'm never going to be a God-lover, a what, hit-my-knees person? That is not who I am. *I know who I am.* Dmitri is not who I am, he is not he is not he is not. I was Houdini with a stuck padlock, upside down in the East River, working so damn hard to keep myself apart from this experience that my sweat began to compete with my surprising tears.

We all hung on his words as his story traced the rise of

a spoiled only child—spectacular, golden, über-successful, powerful, professional, virile, desired, doted on by wife, children, and numerous mistresses—who then began the inevitable crossover into desperately numb, jailed, penniless, shamed, before finally hitting a classic, awful bottom. We were all on board, sober, drunk, high, addict, newcomer, or, like me, semicasual observer, as Dmitri described the decidedly unglamorous thud of landing in one of these fucked-up metal chairs. And learning humility. And service. Life outside his own immediate needs. The gap closed suddenly and gracelessly between them and me, and I felt something slip in me, in my ego, like a herniated disk. Equal parts confused and suddenly in pain, I slumped in my chair, exhaling as if I'd been holding my breath for twenty minutes, and thought:

Goddammit.

A slowly evolving combination of mantra and birth contractions.

Goddammit.

I'm suddenly aware of my posture—slumping lower as if, vertebra by vertebra, I were transforming into the class idiot, a humiliated pudding in a metal folding chair. I begin looking for a way out of there without tripping on thirty pairs of legs. That isn't going to happen. Trapped.

I know—even through my high, my pride, my numb, I know—that I am Dmitri on Christmas Day. We are obviously different, but his story speaks of the kind of person we *all* are in this room. Everybody is the same, whether homeless or, like me, thinking they're still pulling the wool over the eyes of friends, family, coworkers, and the rest of the world.

At the end of his talk, he asks all newcomers to stand. I don't need to, of course, because I'm not a newcomer; I'm a *visitor*. As if he could hear me thinking, he says that if there are people who see themselves in his story but aren't sure they're addicts, there's a pamphlet on the literature table in the back of the room called, naturally, *Am I an Addict?* and inside there's a fairly exhaustive quiz. If you check *yes* to more than half of the questions, he says, you can stop denying the truth and admit who you are. So while Jen goes off to mingle after the meeting, I sneak off to the back of the room and fill out the checklist. It's less curiosity and more avoidance. I just don't want to talk to *any* of these people.

"Do you lose time from work due to drinking or drugs?" *Well, sure, but it's not like it's a big deal; the atmosphere at the shelter is really informal.* But whatever atrophied bit of honesty there is in me guides my pencil to check "yes."

"Have you ever manipulated or lied to a doctor to obtain prescription drugs?" *Yeah, but that doesn't*—check.

Goddammit.

"Have you ever stolen from your friends and family so you could buy drugs or alcohol?" Check.

"Has your using ever cost you a relationship?" Check.

"Has your using ever cost you a job?" Check.

Goddamn fuck.

I answer yes to every question but one, and that's only because there were enough people at that party when the cops busted it that they didn't bother running after me to arrest me. Putting pencil to check box each time feels like a root canal. There's no squirming out of the dentist's chair this time.

I went to a meeting the next night. And the next. And surprised myself by going to yet another. I was making friends, not being judged, which was an amazing thing. When you realize that you've hit bottom, you do plenty of judging all by yourself; the people I met at meetings all seemed to know that and offered an emotional oasis. Jen was also pushing me, and I wanted to impress her—to show her that I could do anything I wanted to do. I wanted her to see that I was strong, which is ironic because really what you're doing by going to these meetings is showing your brokenness to the world and to other broken people

It was during my fourth meeting, on November 23, 2002, that Dmitri kept hammering at me, "Jackson, let me come over to your house, listen, it'll be painless, I'll take all your stuff, and once you get rid of your stuff, you're on the road, come on man, make the commitment to be one of us." And that night I just felt worn down. Dmitri was a verbal jackhammer, and I couldn't think of a better reason to keep fighting the onslaught. I couldn't come up with a better argument to stay high.

So I said, "Okay. Tomorrow. When Beth is at work. I can't take her . . . look."

That night I got raucously high and raucously drunk and raucously pilled up; if I was going to go out, I was going to go out in style. I picked up an eighth of the finest smoke in Boulder, I had plenty of Klonopin, I opened two bottles of wine, I got some coke, even a few tabs of Ecstasy that I discovered in a mournful but desperately spastic scavenger hunt. And I did it all. When the boys came over the next morning, there was nothing left but vessels—pipes, bongs, mirrors, corkscrews—and I shook, while Benny looked on, impassive, as they took away the only confirmation I had that I existed, in the same way that some people collect old newspapers until they make a rats' maze of their homes or others don't throw away their ex-girlfriend's sweatshirt. But they were absolutely right to get rid of all of it. I've seen people relapse because they happen to have a pipe that had sentimental value and they threw it in their closet, and one day they found it. Besides, Dmitri and his friends didn't find the Klonopin I'd hidden in several places around the apartment. I was reasonable about it. They were in plain view, for the most part, in prescription bottles. Prescription bottles for chronic heartburn meds, but still . . . Classic addict "don't ask/don't tell." And then he was gone, toting a surprisingly large garbage bag, like the anti-Santa, and within minutes I began to panic.

The next day was like the worst acid trip imaginable. I was pelted with images and semifamiliar actions—talking to clients, adopters, and other administrators with my studied togetherness—while floating out of body and making fun of my own mouth for the bullshit spilling out of it. "Yes, ma'am, that dog is really cute." *Seriously? Cute? When did I become a character in a rom-com on Lifetime?* "Would you like to take him for a walk?" *God, this hurts this hurts this hurts now. This can't be the dope. Do I need a fucking doctor?* "Yes, we've vaccinated him." *I am a pathetic human being.* I was drowning in nudity, shame, and judgment. There was a self-conscious pause between opposite ends of my conversations with everyone that day, like the awful echo that would greet my voice when wishing my grandmother happy birthday through the transcontinental soup-can phone connection. (I still have a complex about speaking foreign languages because of hearing my awful Hungarian echoing back at me.)

Late in the day, though, I was working on a particularly traumatized cat, doing a bit of therapeutic cat touch, massaging his scruff and shoulders, giving gentle traction to his tail, and my ego was so battered that my boundaries simply washed away. I felt I could go deeper with him. Starting with soft, blinking eye contact, telling him this level of trust was good, I put one hand at the base of his head and one at the base of his tail. I relaxed and expected nothing more, just hoped he would allow himself to connect with me. And all of a sudden I felt the energy of the earth come through my feet, out of my hands, through his body, into the air, and back to the earth, and I could tell he felt it, too. There was no way I could've been awake enough to perceive this only twenty-four hours before. And *this* was the reason I unconsciously chose asleep; *this* is not a safe place—*this* is what *source* feels like, the great cosmological wall outlet I had stuck my finger into. And I took someone with me and asked him, silently, in a language of compromised gestures, to accept. This could have only happened to someone coming back to life, allowing his synapses to fire and his emotions to grow their own nerve endings.

It was my first moment of serenity in years, and I held on to it desperately for the next ninety days (the first stage in recovery) with every molecule of my being. There's no willpower in the world that could have gotten me through that first ninety days on my own—none. But every time I went to a meeting, somebody would talk about being sober, and I would look at him and think, *I want what he has, I want the promise of being whole again, the promise of being creative again, the promise of feeling any- and everything again.* And when I got home, Benny was there to remind me, a breathing symbol of every battered animal soul that had passed through my hands in the shelter years as if he, too, were saying *I want the promise of being whole again, and I need you to be whole to give it to me.* The way I found that promise, for both of us, was to commit—emotionally, physically, and spiritually—to the job I had with animals. I never did find that kind of blind, unflinching spirituality displayed by politicians and winners of the Heisman Trophy as, through tear-filled eyes, they thank their moms, their coaches, and their Lord and Savior; but in the continuing and unpretty flailing-about that we call spirituality, this call became my higher power.

I was two weeks clean when Danielle took me into her office at the shelter and fired me. She was two sentences into explaining the economic reality of the new building and the cutbacks needed to . . . staffing priorities . . . donation levels . . . and my mind was filled with the story about the guy who lives in a state of panic about taking his beloved but absolutely filthy jalopy to the carwash because he has a secret fear that the dirt is what's holding it together. Maybe the dirt was what had been holding me together. When I got clean, there would be no more dirt, and I would fall apart. Everybody who gets sober knows that there is a period of time where it's like your legs were cut off and you just have to learn how to walk again.

My work at the shelter had already gotten me press in

the form of newspaper, TV, and radio; all I had to do now was follow the path. The problem was that the path was a crooked and ridiculous one. Very few people in the country without veterinary degrees were making a halfway decent living being cat-behavior consultants. But Danielle told me the shelter would take care of me—in the months to come, their referrals would be my main source of income.

I walked out of the shelter, blinking against the sun and the shock. I paused with my hand on the handle of my car door. Sighed and bowed my head. Suddenly paranoid that someone was watching me grieve, I switched gears and, with all of the "act as if" confidence I could muster, got in and slammed the door, ready as I'd ever be to set up shop on my own.

Completely
With (out)

I t was on the way to my first consult after getting fired that
my truck broke down.

Within a week after I left the shelter, my computer literally melted into the floor, and I was driving from the
nicotine-stained, windowless apartment of the agoraphobic
genius who had said he would try to repair it (he had gone
from saying, "This is a pretty easy fix" over the phone to
"This is a serious problem" when I dropped it off). I had just
spent something like $1,600 on the truck a week before I
was let go from the shelter, and the mechanic warned me
before starting, "I can't promise you this is gonna fix it,
and if you hear this kind of 'ka-ka-BANG!,' then you know
that it didn't." I was white-knuckling the drive, sweating
through the calculations of how much I was going to spend
on the computer versus how much I stood to make on this

consult, and, oh yeah, *panicking* about the consult itself, when the truck made the ka-ka-BANG. The whole car just seized up. As I coasted to the side of the interstate, the cross fade began.

The truck slows to the point where I can hear individual pieces of gravel crunching under the wheels, my emotional fever accelerating, its rising tempo and volume morbidly familiar from the days when my sanity had slipped from view. The corpse of that 1987 Ford will never be driven again, I realize, so figuring it might as well serve some purpose, I use it as a safe place to lose my shit altogether. The momentum of tears and heaving convulses me over the wheel and I begin to rip apart everything that isn't nailed down and then, as the fever rises, I'm literally ripping the dashboard to pieces. I pull my legs up and kick the speedometer through the gaps of the steering wheel. I tear the leg of my jeans as they get stuck in the stick shift. Finally, with one exhausted heave, I kick and rip off the metal Bronco logo plate along with the glove compartment door. I want a goddamned souvenir.

Now, in the quiet of my broken mess, I know: This is what it feels like to be completely without.

That morning, I had just had no money and no job. That I could deal with. But now that I had no money, no job, no computer, and no car, I was lost, because, money, job, computer, and car aside, what I really didn't have any more of was life lube—I had nothing to make my existence feel less bone on bone. I was three weeks' clean. I wasn't even remotely equipped to deal with the situation I found myself in. When addicts, in the midst of an intervention, start listing all of the important things they had to do in the next two weeks that would make going to rehab impossible, this is what they're trying to avoid. We know absolutely fuckall about finding faith on the other side of fear, desolation, and the endless bottom. We just see pain and run headlong in the other direction.

On the side of the road, crying, I called my father. "How did you do it?" I said raggedly. "You came to this country with no English. You built a business from scratch, you supported a new family while your in-laws were sitting on the sidelines, just waiting for you to fail. How did you do it?"

Silence.

"There was a certain point in every day," he finally said, "especially in the beginning, where I knew that every missed sale was a bill unpaid. I lost a sale every day. I got one every day. My English was terrible. And the thing that could pay my rent was in someone else's hands, the customer that I saw earlier. Could I call them at 9:00 at night while I chewed my fingernails? No. I had to give up. I come from war, fear, no food on the table. I was here, I was all in. I learned to believe that it *would* get better tomorrow. What choice did I have? What choice do you have?"

"OK."

"Now," he said, like the grizzled trainer icing his fighter down between rounds of getting his ass kicked and ears chewed off by Mike Tyson, "that's what you do later tonight, when you have time to lick your wounds. Right now, you have a cat who needs you. Get your ass down there and do what you do!"

So I did.

I spent the taxi ride cleaning myself up from the aftermath of my tantrum. My jeans had begun the day with that oh-so-fashionable rip in the knee, and once they had snagged on the gear shift, they became a slit skirt, leaving very little imagination as to the color of my boxers. So much for hiding my freak flag—it was coming out, increasingly sweat-stained, whether invited or not. I sat in the taxi backseat, repeating my new mantra, the serenity prayer: "Higher Power, grant me the serenity to accept the things I cannot change, the courage to change the things I can and the wisdom to know the difference." I caught myself hitting the imaginary gas pedal and death gripping the imaginary wheel at 10 and 2. *Not* used to being a passenger. But as I was to learn in the recovery meeting rooms, whenever given the wheel to the car, addicts will invariably drive it into the wall or off the cliff. Or rip the fucking thing limb from limb.

Cat Daddy

· · ·

When I finally got to the client's house, I was scared shitless. It had been one thing to go to somebody's apartment as
a shelter employee and work with a cat. If my advice somehow made the cat worse and his guardian ended up bringing him back to the shelter, I knew that I had been going
above and beyond in the first place, and would be able to
take care of the cat in the shelter, advocate for him, and help
behaviorally prep him for a new home. Now that I no longer
worked at the shelter, though, I had no guarantee in terms of
my "pull." If I made a mistake, this cat could, most likely
would, enter the system and possibly—probably—die.

Add to that the fact that, where an unsuccessful consult
used to mean I shrugged off the ego blow, chalked one up to
being a student, and went into work the next day, now an
unsuccessful consult would be lethal to a new business in
terms of word of mouth. I wouldn't be able to pay my rent.
Or feed Benny and Velouria. Or myself.

Like I said: scared shitless.

I was tattered and torn, and somehow some black oily
substance had autographed streaks on my clothing and, as
I wouldn't find out till I got home, on my face, too. With a
deep breath I realized that my attempt at marshaling my
forces was simply a joke that my higher power alone was
laughing at, and I said the serenity prayer again, this time

with an addendum that I still use and modify every day: "Higher Power, grant me the serenity and selfless clarity to bring peace to Smoky, Donna, and her family." One more breath, and I rang the bell.

"His name is Smoky," Donna began once we had sat down, "but we call him Trouble these days."

"I understand," I said. "That's why I'm here." Deep breath. "Now, I usually start by asking the client to tell me what's been going on," I lied, praying that she wouldn't point out she'd already told me everything via e-mail, because I'd left the printout in the beat-up, broke-down remains of the Bronco.

"He's just become so aggressive," she said, her voice thick with frustration. "He didn't use to be like this. He just attacks people completely at random now. And he's so big it gets really frightening."

"How big is big?"

"Eighteen pounds."

Of course, I thought. *You couldn't throw me a cat who was peeing on something. Today of all days. Really? This is going to hurt. I just know it. At least I'm dressed for a fight.*

Smoky was apparently, to hear Donna tell the story, very much like Benny—which was the first hint of good news I had heard all day, albeit in a pretty backhanded way. As change was presented to him, Smoky got more and more unpredictable. First as they moved into this house, then as the family continued to grow. There were six-month-old twins in the nursery and two other children, aged three and six. Every time something shifted, Smoky crept away from being the loving cat Donna and her husband had adopted as a kitten and toward being, as she called him, "the spawn of the devil," at least according to the in-laws, extended family, friends, and neighbors.

And there was the rub . . . Smoky never laid a paw on Donna, her husband, or the kids; it was everybody else who lit Smoky's quick-burning fuse and brought his claws of judgment down on them.

"He tends to hang out at the top of the stairs," Donna said when I finally began my tour of the territory. Sure enough, there he was on a landing halfway up the *Gone with the Wind* staircase, a beautiful but, sure enough, menacing gray cat with green eyes. He was fixed on me and nerve-rackingly still.

Even though Smoky's energy literally gave me a chill up my spine, like my own fight or flight instincts were being activated, I was present enough to remember that you have to enter feline territory with quiet confidence. Otherwise they feel it, and it has a fingernail-on-the-chalkboard vibe. I walked up to him on the landing and very gently said, "Hey, Smoky," in the voice that I had spent a few years perfecting, the one I knew melted cats' hearts. Again, one of the duties of the cat detective is exploring the totality of your vocal range, and finding, for each individual cat, where in the accepted range their sweet spot lies, where they become receptive. This technique has been especially helpful in cases where I try to establish a line of trust with a feral cat, where hand contact, at least at first, is impossible.

Smoky just held his gaze and I held my breath a bit. I adjusted my approach. I figured just coming at him from a straight line was a mistake; he might perceive it to be an offensive move, one that left no escape routes. So I stood on the floor off to the side of the banister, and said again, "Hey, Smoky, hey bud . . ."

And Smoky *flung* himself from that landing, which was probably twelve feet in the air, directly onto my head. Donna was right; he was eighteen pounds of solid muscle, and when he hit me it was like getting punched in the face with a fist. A fist with claws. And teeth.

I stayed surprisingly calm, though, as I was having the ever-loving shit kicked out of me. While the slow motion carnage unfolded, Donna's voice a dull yet incredibly high-octave scream in the distance, I realized that if I was ever shot at close range, I could stay present (and conscious) enough to apply my own tourniquet. I spun slowly toward the stairs, taking the time to unhook Smoky's front claws from my skin (one of those eternal cat frustrations is that it's the most aggressive cats who have the sharpest claws, because nobody has the guts to get near the things to clip them). In the meantime, he entered full-on vampire mode;

dealing with his claws had been one thing, but getting his teeth out of my neck was another thing altogether. I scruffed him and crouched down, dipping him like my partner in a perverse tango. I wanted to bring him to a vulnerable position, with his back to the floor, so he would instinctively release his hold on me to see where he was in relation to a potential fall to earth. The fugue state broken, he was "in his skin" again long enough to abandon the fight and run instead. Run right back to that spot at the top of the stairs to resume his job.

As soon as the tornado of shit-kicking was over and I knelt bleeding on Donna's marble floor, the pressure eased up. I mean, unless the shoe bomber was hiding in the pantry, I felt safe in assuming that I had just experienced the cherry on top of the most screwed-up few days of my life. I understood Smoky better now than I possibly could have beneath the miasma of career panic and strange aggressive cat dread I had felt minutes before. And he had proven, beyond a shadow of a doubt, who was boss here.

"See? That's what happens," Donna said while fetching me some damp washcloths. "Nobody is remotely safe in this house!" She was beginning to hyperventilate, looking at the damage he had caused me. I was telling her it was OK, to breathe, but I'm sure that meant little coming from me at that point. It was beyond important that I get cleaned up and stop the blood coming through my clothes. This energy in a room, the beginning of the avalanche triggered by the realization of the guardian's worst fears about a cat, had become a very familiar one; after a few disasters, I knew now what to do: Get out of it; find a silver lining. Otherwise, Smoky's fate, along with the other cats like him, was already sealed.

The thing is, it didn't bother me that I was oozing blood. I was just relieved not to be thinking about the fact that my life depended on the results of this consult. I was dealing with Smoky, the cat, the troubled individual, and *that* was something I knew how to do. I was dealing with Donna, her tearful, all-consuming stress. *That* was something I knew how to do. I didn't have any questions about my ability. This was just one being relating to other beings, all of us in the same vulnerable space, and it came naturally. I felt, despite what must have been my absolutely hideous beat-up appearance, that I was working in my wheelhouse.

"Well," I said—emerging from the bathroom as cleaned up as I could get, tissue all over my neck, head, and chest like I was the victim of the worst manscaping accident ever—"it's pretty clear that he's guarding something upstairs." I smiled, as if to convey to Donna that this happened to me all the time (which it didn't), and that I was fine (which I wasn't, not even close). "Let's go take a look at what's up there."

Be a Cat Detective

My experiences have taught me really important skills in terms of remedying behavior issues:

1. **Disengage**

   The first step as a cat guardian who is "at the end of your rope," is climb back up a bit. Nothing will get solved while you're spinning out over the problem. Disengage, become a true observer, even if it is your house, your body, or your sleep that is affected. Remember your cat is not doing ANYTHING to spite you.

2. **Journal!**

   Nothing your cat does is random. He is built for routine. Chronicle your activities and his activities. When does he use the litter box? When does he act out? What time do you wake up and come home and how does the energy change in the house? Noting the details is indispensable, especially as you try to work out a behavioral plan of action.

We started up the stairs. This time, I would not overthink the approach, and I would absolutely ignore Smoky. Just invent something to talk about as we passed him so all he heard was an ease in the cadence of my voice. Of course, I also had Donna lead the way, so as to mitigate any possible territorial stress he was feeling. As we talked about it, it turned out that this final insane behavioral turn hadn't started until the new babies had come into the house. And as soon as I saw their room, just to the right of the landing, everything made sense quickly. We all know that the nature of cats is a territorial one; Smoky, as more children arrived in the territory, recognized them as über-important components to the safety of the whole; he would assume this "protector" persona, and, sure enough, *it worked*! Strangers kept their distance from that all-important seat of the territory. With the arrival of twins, the combination of his perceived job coupled with the territorial overload had simply proven too much. He was stressed out, and as a result, he could no longer inhibit his actions.

We started by letting Smoky know that, in fact, *every* room was important. That might sound counterintuitive now, but I thought that if everything was equal, the castle would be, to a degree, indefensible—and he would have to release his tight grip of control over it and perhaps surrender.

We took one of the twins' blankets and rubbed it all over

the place. I brought the rocking chair and Donna brought the babies downstairs so she could nurse and tell stories in the middle of the living room instead of doing it in the nursery. They had been feeding Smoky upstairs, too, so we brought his food downstairs, brought his toys down, spread everything out. And finally Smoky could say, "Ahh, that's right, there's my food and my water. Oh, I smell the baby right here. Litter boxes with my scent spread throughout. Great, that's mine, too. All of this is mine, and there's no Alamo to defend." By the time we were done, we could see Smoky relaxing in front of our eyes. He was a different cat.

When I got home, I looked in the mirror and the gift of recovery unfurled, because I could remind myself that I had *something* after all. I had a bed to get into, a door to lock, a window that looked out over the beautiful Flatirons. I had a remarkable experience that I was sober enough to remember and feel grateful for despite the oozing and throbbing souvenirs. Gratitude was a new feeling; I actually felt grateful that I got to experience and, better, feel the things I did in the two previous days. I moved through pain and didn't let it turn into suffering. Smoky had given me not just scars that I carried for quite a few years but also invaluable lessons past the swirling, ominous, and ultimately misunderstood energy. He taught me how to approach people like Donna better. This is a lesson none of us can forget. You can be a cat *god* and it doesn't mean shit at the end of the day if you don't have equal sympathy for the humans. Without their buy-in, you're a cat god surrounded by dead or turned-out cats.

It was a good day after all. Go figure.

The Problem
with Letters and
the Bum Within

Meanwhile, Benny was doing his level best to make my life at home as difficult as possible.

After I had told Beth that I was getting clean, she stopped talking to me—she needed to get loaded just as much as I needed to sober up, and it pissed her off. The way using playmates see it, not only are you turning your back on them, you are implying that they are somehow broken, diseased. And that brings the fight out in people. When the first of my running buddies had found the twelve steps years before, I openly mocked him as "Jesus Freak," even "coward." His defection, in a backhanded way, put the rest of us up against the wall. And just like feral cats, when cornered, we struck back with a vengeance. And now so did Beth.

I knew that in order to commit to my recovery I was going to have to abandon this friendship, hopefully just until the dust settled, because living with that wreckage amid the wreckage around us was not a healthy thing to do. This meant that Beth took over most of our apartment and I, for the sake of expedience (I wanted to avoid conflict) stayed in my bedroom. After a month, I couldn't take it anymore—neither could the cats—and I called a realtor.

"What do you think of this place?" she asked when she showed me the apartment.

It's too big, I thought. It was a two-bedroom apartment where I had my own office, a big bedroom, a big living room, a dining room. *I'm really uncomfortable here.*

"Mountain view, great price," said Jen. "He'll take it." I could only nod in wan agreement.

Meanwhile, I had no furniture—I was proud of the sort of Spartan lifestyle I had led, and in a nod to my Roma heritage, my life could still fit into my car. I had left my useless futon at the old place. The couch had been Beth's. I didn't own a TV. Nothing. But because I was clean I had more money than I had in the past, so I went on a buying spree. Trips to Target to get things I had never thought of before, like freaking silverware, a toothbrush holder, a plunger. Of course, the cats had everything they could have needed. I kept waking up trying to figure out where the frying pan was. My dad, sensing my helplessness, flew out to help. He and I went to a country auction and bought an entire set of house furniture for $400. My big splurge was a brand-new king-size bed. Even so, I didn't put any art on the glaringly, migrainishly white walls for six months, I think because I was living with a fear of commitment—like your lover giving you a drawer in the dresser that you never put so much as a pair of socks in. I couldn't bring myself to put my roots down and claim the place as my own.

Slowly but surely, though despite my discomfort, I adjusted to the move. Benny, on the other hand, showed no interest in adjusting to anything, because he didn't know what to do with the world today when it looked *at all* different than yesterday. This is something those who live with felines know all too well: cats like stability. Once they see things arranged in an acceptable way, they tend to be unhappy with change.

But if cats are creatures of habit, Benny was a creature of absolute rigidity.

He made his discomfort clear immediately after the move, by picking three different spots and peeing on them as if they were made of litter. But it was okay, I told myself, because I knew how to deal with this.

The first thing was not to panic, because all panic does is escalate the problem. (This is the first mistake that people make in situations like this: the cats lose their pee and the humans lose their shit.) So after *not panicking*, I got three litter boxes and put them in the places where he'd been peeing. The idea is that once you put down multiple litter boxes, a cat who's been peeing where you don't want him to can now pee on something that is appropriate and say, "That's right, I smell this, this belongs to me. Next?" Gradually, you move each box toward the place where you want there to be one litter box.

So I set up three litter boxes for Benny in the places he wanted to pee. Instead of trying to get him to do something I wanted him to do, this was very much about embracing compromise and acknowledging his overriding need to reinforce territorial identification in these places. Recognizing that these boxes were smack in the middle of *my* space, even impeding logical walkways, I had a moment of being a litter box baby, whining that what I had to do for him was so invasive, so inconvenient. "Fine," I said to myself in the end; "I'm going to put litter boxes in those places. And I will give it exactly a week. Not a day more." And it worked. Benny started using the litter boxes again within a day.

Of course with Benny I had to know that any celebration would always be mocked. A few days later I moved two of the boxes a couple of feet toward the third, which was in a slightly more human-friendly location, and Benny started peeing everywhere again. I spent days going, "What? What? What the hell is it?" and feverishly thumbing through my inner cat/human dictionary, looking for the answer and not finding it. In this case, the moment of translational discovery was my realization that I'd been moving the boxes too

Don't Be a Litter Box Baby!

- If I told you that your cat would stop peeing all over your house if you added well-placed litter boxes, would you blink? Of course not. So when I tell you that they need to go in socially significant areas (bedroom or dining room, for example), don't turn into a litter box baby! Do you want it on the floor or in the box? I thought so.

- Put a litter box wherever your cat is peeing (or pooping). Now you are giving her an acceptable choice to mark territory; you're giving her the possibility of a positive behavioral outlet.

- As time goes on and the boxes are used with a 100 percent success rate, you can start to shift them toward an area that is more amenable to your lifestyle. But remember, just a few feet a day.

- Finally, when all the boxes are concentrated in the one area, begin to eliminate the extras. Three become two become one—presto! Problem solved.

far. When Benny saw a box that was three feet away from where it had been the day before, he would become disoriented and furious—three feet would be fine for most cats I had known, but was absolutely unacceptable to Benny—and would pee in the same old place again. The trick became finding his "challenge line."

 How Can You Use the Challenge Line?

Even if you have a seemingly well-adjusted cat, there has to be something that challenges them. Why do we want to find it? Two reasons:

1) Meeting challenges means increased self-esteem. Just as you gained confidence the first time you scaled the monkey bars or the day you got your driver's license, so it is with any being. With scaredy-cats, their challenges so often have to do with ownership, or as they perceive it, lack of ownership. Kill the toy, you own that toy and the space in which it was killed. Venture out to a living room full of people and other animals when you're used to hiding under the bed and your confidence zooms as you take your place in the world.

2) The ability to push through challenges lowers stress in times of unforeseen life changes. Not that this is something you want to think about, but if something happens to you, what happens to your cat? If she will only eat a certain brand of food, with this or that sprinkled on top, and then only on odd-numbered days, the stress of having to do something different in, God forbid, a shelter environment might well be insurmountable and she might quit eating.

We owe it to our cats to shake up their routines, to allow them to grow. On the other side of the challenge line is comfort, and although we want them to know that their world and the beings in it are safe, permanent, and friendly, feeling success and pleasure on both sides of the line provides them with a behavioral elasticity that will serve them (and in turn, us) well for their whole lives.

The challenge line is something that became a part of my toolbox from that time on—finding the place where comfort changes to challenge. Think of a child dipping his toes in the pool versus jumping into the water, taking off training wheels, or taking away a blankie or a pacifier. In trying to effect behavioral change, it's totally counterproductive to throw the cat's sense of comfort out the window, to throw her into an ice bath of sorts. She'll push back violently, squirming to be free of the ice again, as Benny did, trying to find the comfort again. So instead, we ask her, every day, to approach challenge, and put one paw over it. The line is suddenly extinguished and moved up. And we start again, always gently assuring her that small challenges are met with great reward on the other side. In this case, I found that if I moved those boxes a few inches each day, Benny could get with the program. Six inches was comfort; a foot, unacceptable challenge. So it came to pass, after my discovery of the challenge line concept, that my apartment was full of litter boxes for three weeks, moving by inches as Benny slept, like I was the litter box version of Santa, until the boxes finally merged into one, in a human-acceptable location.

At the same time as we were dealing with the litter box issue, though, Benny also really started to dominate Velouria. Cats thrive on ownership, and Benny was who he was, so he felt like he needed to overassert himself, to *over-own*. I think the enlarged territory, for once unburdened by closed doors and other cats, led Benny to make sure Velouria knew where she was permitted to stand, sit, and lie, at exactly what times and in what manner. This was his chance, and he wasn't going to waste it. Velouria was not just submissive but scared, so she was always on the run, always looking for a place he couldn't get to, but many times it would end badly for her. It was not a good scene. Velouria, furthermore, didn't do herself any favors, because a cat who runs and makes noise and turns herself into a great little squeaky toy, as she did, is going to get chased. Whenever I let her sleep under the covers with me, which she loved to do, some time during the night Benny would walk across the bed and literally step on her. She would make a noise, and all hell would break loose. He got to a point where he really didn't like her being on the bed at all, so instead of accidentally stepping on her, he would patrol with vigilance to keep her off.

"You guys," I finally said to them—and to myself—"we're going to be together for a long time, and we have to make this work. I'm not going to give either one of you up, but we have to work together."

They looked dubious.

I didn't really want to do too much of anything; site swapping, for example, would mean more closed doors, which I felt in this case would only mean heavier retribution from Benny. This situation provided my first opportunity to solve problems in a large, open "behavioral laboratory" of sorts. There were no outside influences—no roommates, no other cats, no dogs, practically no visitors. The question was, how could I ensure safety on Velouria's end of the equation and confident ownership on Benny's?

Observation of Benny and Velouria led me to the concept

Site Swapping

When cats have met poorly or have had a crazy fight that results in distrust, most often I take them back to square one and reintroduce the cats as if they had never met. One of the initial keys is site swapping.

The cats should never be allowed direct eye contact in the beginning; instead, they get equal access to the territory, but during different times. One gets free reign, one gets the "base camp" (most often the master bedroom). This way, they can each own everything, increasing confidence, and begin to be reintroduced gently, through shared scent, but not tussle over who owns what.

of Tree Dwellers and Bush Dwellers. What I realized was that Velouria always felt more comfortable high up, even when she wasn't threatened. She would leap up to the top of a door frame and then look for the next high-up space to jump to, like Tarzan looking for a vine. Benny, in the meantime, was decidedly more at home when all four paws were on the ground. He had dropped out of cat school before they taught Jumping 101. I chalked it up to his old pelvic injury, though there are all sorts of natural reasons cats can be attracted or restricted to the ground.

It reminded me of watching big-cat hunting behavior. Lions and many of their cousins crouch low in the brush, moving almost noiselessly among the reeds. Sometimes they eat their kill right there in the middle of the plain. These cats show their confidence on the ground, hence bush dwellers. Other big cousins, most notably the leopard, will kill with equal precision on the ground, but then drag their prey into a tree, where hyenas and other scavengers will more than likely leave them alone. They will eat, nap, and survey the vast territory from the safety of their tree houses; leopards are tree dwellers.

Sure, adapting these behaviors to house cats involves healthy doses of liberal interpretation and imagination. But the upshot was that I had a new tool, a new way of categorizing the cats I met, assessing their confidence (or lack thereof), and devising solutions based on those needs. And the cool thing was that this could be accomplished without robbing these cats of their individuality. In the case of my cats, knowing that Velouria was a tree dweller and Benny was a bush dweller meant I could design an environment pleasing to both while doubling the volume of the perceived territory.

I used kitty sills, condos, run-of-the-mill Home Depot shelving units, and turned what had been a one-lane dirt road into a cat superhighway. Benny and Velouria could, if

Tree Dweller or Bush Dweller?

It's important to note that just because a cat is a tree or a bush dweller, it doesn't mean that one is a better option than the other. For instance, some cats like heights. They derive confidence from these locations. Many cats I've known have been chased to, say, the top of the fridge, and they become too scared to come down so they pee, poop, and eat up there. The same can go for bush dwellers, those who seek floor-level safe havens like a closet or under a bed.

- Observe your cats nonjudgmentally. Are they confident or nonconfident bush or tree dwellers?
- If they're confident, build your space to accommodate.
- If they're nonconfident, use the challenge line to show them a fuller world filled with brave choices.

they chose, stay completely out of each other's way so as to establish a system of time-sharing that cats, no matter how large the group, can be masters at. I kept Velouria safe and I gave them both places to go where they would be able to claim different areas of the house. But I didn't enforce a separation, and over time, depending on Benny's stress level, he just let Velouria be.

One of the main reasons I didn't become a professional before I did, during the long spell when I was contemplating leaving the shelter, was that I didn't have any letters after my name (well, that and the fact that I was incapacitated). I couldn't call myself Jackson Galaxy, VMD, DVM, AVSAB, CAAB, IAABC, or CABC. I didn't go to school for what I was professing to do, and this made me afraid to go out in the world, because I was terrified of being wrong . . . and, worse, being judged.

What made it worse was that there were definitely issues on which I disagreed, sometimes vehemently, with the people who *did* have letters after their names. One of the earliest examples I can remember of this was my initial repulsion over the seemingly common act of declawing. It was just common sense to me, no matter what studies I read to the contrary or however many vets and veterinary behav-

The Cat Superhighway

Take advantage of every conceivable nook and cranny and survey point, from under the couch to the top of the bookcase. Be imaginative about how you can accommodate your feline tree or bush dweller.

- Especially if you have multiple cats, catering to the bush and tree dwellers means they can own the world on their own terms.
- Not competing for doors and wall space on the floor means less traffic. Build more lanes for different kinds of feline commuters and you'll have fewer traffic snarls, literally!
- Remember, whatever you build, including spaces for litter boxes, needs to have multiple entrance points. Also, more exits on the highway mean less chance for ambush and more for happy coexistence.

iorists I consulted, that the result to both cats' bodies and their psyches was more often than not catastrophic. I knew, just watching a cat walk across the floor, that she'd been declawed. Her gait seemed unnatural. I was recording more and more litter box issues having to do with box aversion from declawed cats. The number of "botch jobs" was astounding. And even worse, those cats with tendonectomies, where guardians' vets convinced them that the surgery was a humane alternative to declawing, angered me to no end. Those poor guys had to walk around with no power of retraction over their claws, getting them snagged on carpeting. And the "professionals" I sought the advice of would, with equal parts self-righteous anger and condescension, assure me that there were no studies that backed up any such assertion, that I was being anthropomorphic and was failing if I ever wanted to pursue the "science" of animal behavior. I'm happy to say that declawing is now illegal in twenty-seven countries, earning prison sentences in some, and in many American cities. But there are still vets and guardians all over the place who see no problem with it.

Now, fifteen years later, I've come to believe that I'm part of a different generation of professional animal people who come to the field from a different direction, one that offers equally informed discourse but from a fresh perspective. At that time, however, the only thing that I knew was that I was a fraud; I felt like I had stolen someone else's identity and I was using it liberally, knowing, with a true addict's mix of dread and excitement, that at any moment I would be caught.

After going to a seminar in Denver given by a respected

Don't Declaw Your Cat!

It's easy to think of declawing a cat as just permanently clipping her nails, but nothing could be less accurate.

Imagine somebody cutting off all your fingers just below the first knuckle, and then having to go through life like that. That's much closer to what a declawed cat experiences. Declawing can cause physical, behavioral, and emotional problems for years to come.

If your cat is scratching things you don't want her to scratch, here are some things you can do:

- make sure she has satisfactory scratching surfaces that *aren't* furniture
- instead of old carpet, try sisal or corrugated cardboard
- try Soft Paws: covers you can put on her claws to keep her scratching from doing any damage

animal behaviorist, I went up to her, full of relief that I wasn't alone on this island. It wasn't even that I wanted her advice on how to establish myself as a behaviorist. I just wanted to talk about cats. It was like the first time I met another musician at a twelve-step meeting and we ended up talking about *Sgt. Pepper's* versus *Pet Sounds*. It was a three-hour talkgasm, a friendly face in a foreign land.

"Hey," I said, stars in my eyes, "I'm in the process of going into this field, and I'd love to have a conversation with you." I went on, for just long enough to realize that I was just speaking, doing that "Jesus, she's not saying a word and I want to show her I'm smart and the silence is making me sweat" type of prattle. As I talked, the expression on her face gradually went from sure-I'd-be-happy-to-autograph-your-copy-of-my-book to what-the-*fuck*-is-that-floating-in-my-soup. "And so I guess I thought I'd just . . ." I couldn't continue, not in the face of that stony wall.

"It's not something you can just decide you're good at," she finally said in a voice that would have given me frostbite if it could have. And then she turned her back on me and started talking to somebody else.

I don't know whether she felt threatened by me literally—in a sea of sweater vests and horn-rimmed rapture, maybe she thought I was going to steal something—but later that week somebody sent me a link to a post on her Web site from the day of the seminar that said, "ANYBODY can call themselves a cat behaviorist. BEWARE."

I had let her reload the double-barrel fear/doubt shotgun. And from that point forward, I didn't call myself a cat behaviorist. I didn't want her to get mad at me and ultimately reveal me as the fake I was. So I called myself a "cat behavior consultant." And as time went on I called myself a lot of other things, but initially, at least, calling myself Cat Boy or Cat Daddy or cat translator or cat shrink was just a lighthearted way of avoiding the embarrassing truth that there was a part of me that had heard her and believed that I wasn't qualified to do the job. It wasn't enough to be an empathic being, it wasn't enough to know a lot about cats, to understand them on a fundamental level. I began to cover my tattoos when I went to people's houses; I took out my earrings. "I want my clients to pay attention to their cats and not my look," I said to myself, but what I really meant was, "I want my clients not to notice that I don't know the four-syllable words you have to know to do this work."

When I was very young, I used to go to work with my dad, watching in awe as he made deals in his unsteady English and just as often ripped somebody a new asshole. He had a sign on the wall near his desk. The walls were that dark wood paneling that was everywhere in the early '70s. The sign was driftwood, the kind of plaque that was abundant on every boardwalk from Coney Island to Atlantic City. Next to a hobo's face were carved the words, "Selling is like shaving—if you don't do it every day, you're a *bum*!"

My dad always said to me that as long as I was happy, he

was happy. But now, in the early days of punching my own clock, clean and sober for the first time in memory, completely out of any comfort zone I'd ever known, I reverted to that kid—I hung on my dad's approval, and felt like I was the face on that stained driftwood. From across the country he knew, I imagined, that I was sleeping too late, not presenting myself like a professional.

The problem, or the blessing, depending on how you look at it, was that the image I had spent a lifetime crafting was not coverable, not erasable, not shavable. When I actually worked for my dad, starting the summer after my sophomore year in high school, the struggle was apparent. I was an inveterate people-pleaser, I wanted my dad to be happy with me, but still I HAD to fly my freak flag. That summer I got my ear pierced; my first serious girlfriend did it with a safety pin and ice, of course.

"What the hell have you done to yourself?" asked my father when he saw me.

"What does it look like?"

"Well, you're not working with that in your ear."

So I took it out in the morning and put it back in during lunch, then back out, then back in at the end of the day. I was a bleeding, oozing mess. It made no sense to me—how could my dad be fine with the blood running down my neck but find a stupid gold stud unacceptable?

Back then I hadn't given a shit—within weeks I was making earrings out of matchbox cars. Now, though, with my dad's perceived entrepreneurial judgment on one side, the well-known behaviorist's scorn on the other, and nothing in the middle except my missing letters, I didn't know what to do.

But then Jean Hofve came into my life with her letters and her approval, to let me know that everything would be okay.

Two weeks after the shelter had moved into our brand-spanking-new building, we experienced a tremendous outbreak of upper-respiratory infection in our cat population. The cats were in serious trouble, because the infection meant that they couldn't smell their food, and the fact that they couldn't smell their food meant that they weren't eating. At all. We had feeding tubes in most of them, and I had a crew of cat volunteers, but despite our best efforts and intentions, they couldn't do much good, and I couldn't do much good. I mean, what were we going to do, hang out around the cats and love the infection away?

And then somebody told me about this veterinarian, Dr. Jean, who had a line of holistic remedies called Spirit Essences. "You should ask her to formulate something for the cats," he said, and because we were in a desperate place—these cats were starving to death—I did.

"Just tell your volunteers," she said over the phone, "as many times a day as they walk into that isolation area, just put it on the cats, mist the area, put it in their water."

And the cats got better.

Fast.

I tried to justify it, because this might as well have been something cooked up in a witch's cauldron. "It must be the fact that we're touching them with intention," I said.

"Well, that's possible—it is the nature of vibrational medicine," said Jean, "but minus the explanations, flower essences just work."

That was our first contact, and after that it seemed like everybody was telling me randomly that I needed to work with this woman. I'd finish her name before they got it out, with a semiweary nod. It's like hearing a song you might have just ignored before as background noise and then you're hearing it everywhere. "You and she just see cats and their needs in the same way," one of the shelter workers told me.

When I was "cut back" six months later, suddenly out of a "normal" job, my ass on the couch trying to figure out how to feed Benny and Velouria, it turned out that people had been telling *her* she needed to meet *me*, too. Virtu-

The Importance of Intent

Cats are SO energetically sensitive. A pinnacle manifestation of vibrational energy between beings is touch.

- Why be careless with your power? Every time you bring touch to a being (especially when there is no common spoken language), you have the power to choose a healing message.
- Center yourself with a simple message—for example, "I bring you calm," "I bring you peace." If nothing else, it brings *you* peace and calm which helps to bring wellness to the recipient.
- You can use Spirit Essences or even some hydrosol-based essential oils to act as an energetic conductor for this type of exercise.

ally at the same time as I was let go, she walked away from her $75,000-a-year practice. And a few days after that, literally as I walked in the door of a monthly networking potluck for animal professionals in the area, the hostess of the party, our mutual friend and animal communicator Kate

Solisti, said, "Oh, finally—Jackson, this is Jean, Jean, this is Jackson."

"Oh, my God, it's YOU!" we said in unison.

"We have important work to do," said Jean.

And ten minutes later we had decided to go into business with each other.

Little Big Cat was born out of our deep desire to keep cats in their homes, keep them from becoming part of the statistics that tell us that more than six million cats die in shelters every year. Jean and I had both worked in shelters, and we'd both been forced to euthanize healthy cats. Little Big Cat was created to offer another road—a way through and out of problems.

The mind-body approach was the first concept we developed, although we didn't have a name for it at the time. It was obvious that this was where our strengths intersected: the physical *and* behavioral aspects of a single situation. Jean and I wanted to take the normal, everyday relationship between people and cats to the next level: an enhanced, deeper bond. We knew that if people understood their cats better, knew what the instincts and evolutionary forces were that shaped feline behavior, not only would they be less frustrated with behaviors that were seemingly odd (but actually totally normal), they would develop an admiration of and fascination with those forces.

The name of our company emphasized the essential big cat nature—tiger, lion, leopard—that's still present in the housecat. Domestication is something of a challenge to the cat; although ancient peoples took cats into their homes and hearts, their social life with humans has been very much love/hate since then, and it is much more recent in the cat's history than any other domestic animal that we finally "brought in" for good. Our "little cats" have a core of "big cat" within them (as I'd noticed with the idea of tree and bush dwellers) and so they have very similar needs in terms of behavior and health.

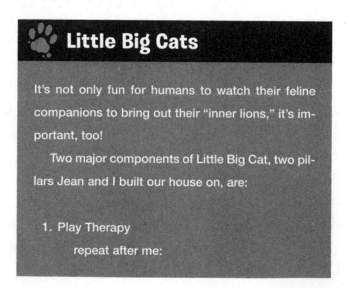

Little Big Cats

It's not only fun for humans to watch their feline companions to bring out their "inner lions," it's important, too!

Two major components of Little Big Cat, two pillars Jean and I built our house on, are:

1. Play Therapy

    repeat after me:

HUNT

CATCH

KILL

EAT

GROOM

SLEEP

This is the natural life of our little predators. If they can't hunt, your play sessions must be geared toward mimicking this activity both in focus and energy expenditure. Play every day and so many "behavior issues" fall by the wayside!

2. The Catkins Diet (again!)

Aside from the physical benefits, discussed previously, of a carnivorous diet like weight control and coat health, behaviorally, you will notice a difference in your cats as they eat their food in a more evolutionarily connected way. They're more likely to compromise. Try to get your cat to perform a sit with a bowl of kibble versus a bowl of meat as a reward. Which one wins?

We would walk into a house where the cat was peeing out-side of the litter box, and even though at first blush it would seem like a cut-and-dry behavioral issue, something, some pattern in the urination or manner of gait, for example, would seem . . . off. Jean and I would confer, she'd step in to do the proper labs and a nose-tip-to-tail exam, including a total reeducation on what cats needed to eat. And that level of completion overcame my "letter paralysis." What she didn't know about cats' secret life I knew, and what I didn't know about the machine draped over the secret, she did. It was incredibly empowering to know that we were philo-sophically in lockstep and, as a unit, confident and com-plete. Having Jean with me meant that I didn't have to be quite so terrified that this conversation would happen:

"So, Jackson, you say you're a cat expert. What are your credentials?"

"I'm a, um, I have a master's degree."

"Really? In what?"

"Um . . . acting. But it helps! No, really. . . . Wait, where are you going?"

I would have gone to vet school to be a veterinary behav-iorist if my mind worked that way, but it doesn't. Jean would spend twelve hours reading and researching and spilling it back out into an article she was writing. I would just as soon slit my wrists.

What I could do, while waiting for the phone to ring for

our first consult, and with my dad's voice bouncing around in my head, was make my family proud and think like a salesman.

My dad is a salesman. My grandfather on my mother's side was a salesman. My brother is a salesman.

I am not a salesman. The only thing I hate more than selling things is having things sold to me. But I needed to eat, I needed to bring in money somehow. And I also needed, I can see now in retrospect, to legitimize what I was doing in my father's eyes. "You're selling animal holy water?" he would say, half bewildered, but he understood the idea of selling *something*. Being a cat shrink made no sense to him. But selling a bill of goods, whether cats, holistic remedies, or the Brooklyn Bridge, he understood.

Spirit Essences, Jean's and my line of flower remedies that addressed the energetic imbalance underlying animals' emotional, physical, and mental issues—things like separation anxiety, asthma, travel stress, and so on—was the only thing in our lives that smelled like commerce. The amount of money it brought in was almost negligible, but it was at least predictable, so I insisted we fold it into our daily Little Big Cat operations. The only way I could make that happen was basically to assure Jean that I would do *everything* outside the realm of conceptualizing, because after spending five years working this tiny engine all by herself, she was sick of it. If this was going to run up the hill, I had to make it go. We built the Spirit Essences Web site as a complement to the Little Big Cat Web site. LBC was about resources, information, the unbridled enthusiasm we both felt. Spirit Essences was the material outgrowth of the ideal; our chance to have the Ben & Jerry's effect. Two normal people making some seriously good stuff for your animal friends. We started getting orders. Very few at first—an order a day, two if we were extremely lucky. But we put out the will to the universe so that orders would start flooding in.

They didn't.

We made, on average, thirty dollars a day. This was how I defined myself: as a businessman who only made thirty dollars a day. In other words, the fraud continued. We both lived off our credit cards.

Every day I would get one of those plastic USPS buckets that mail comes in, and I would take whatever orders we had gotten in the past twenty-four to forty-eight hours, and put them in that bucket, and bring them to the post office. I'd be standing in line at the end of the day with one or two envelopes, glancing at the other small-business owners with their overflowing buckets.

"Hey, there!" I'd say to the man working the window, pretending I was proud of my pathetic bucket.

He wouldn't answer.

"How's your day been?"

"Mm," he'd grunt. He didn't care and he saw right through me. I got it; it was the post office. AND it was the end of the day.

I would look over at the woman who sold rare books, who would come in with twelve totes destined for the arms of collectors all over the world, I would sheepishly smile at her with my one or two envelopes, she'd look at her watch and I would think to myself, "First you're a pretend behaviorist and now you're a pretend businessman." In two years, not a visit to the post office went by that I didn't want to stick my head in the sand as deeply as possible. Or at the least in my plastic postal bucket. God knows there was room in there.

The first time I filled a bucket, I paraded it in there like some postal peacock. Watching the guy behind the desk send my babies off around the country (and the world!) to the hordes of animal guardians who just wanted a better quality of life for their friends, proudly holding up the line of people who just wanted stamps, shooting a flirtatious glance over to my rare book seller compadre, a look she flirtatiously returned—yes, Virginia, size DOES matter—I felt vindicated. I had a business. Not a hobby, like my parents had insisted music and animals were, but a real-life job.

Jean began to slow down noticeably, sleeping less, showing considerably less of what kept me energized through those really rough beginning years. "I'm like a bulldozer," she had said once, in a friendly conversation early on in our work together. "If you're in my way, I'm not going to notice you. And I'm telling you this now because if you ever get crushed under my wheels, the only thing I'm going to say is, 'Why did you let yourself be caught under them in the first place?'" I remember thinking about this conversation at one point during that time. Her bulldozerness was my rock; she cared not at all about offending people, about tossing off those who moved against us philosophically and wasted our time. When left to my own devices, the approval of every living being was *all* I cared about. She inspired, pushed, and lit me up full of ideas as a cat student. And she was just disappearing.

After a particularly scary night in the ER, it was discovered that Jean had heart disease, that at some point she would need a valve replaced. It explained everything. It helped nothing. I was sympathetic and selfishly terrified. I was doing everything: I was ordering essences, I was buying bottles, I was sterilizing the bottles, I was mixing up the formulas, I was designing the labels and putting them together, and I was filling orders, and this stuff took an insanely long amount of time. I was doing everything by myself except making executive decisions, which, at that point, she would just fight with me about.

This is only part of the story, of course; Jean's work was

beyond instrumental in helping spread our ideas. She wrote so many articles and just gave them away on the Web site. LittleBigCat.com became a bastion of feline idealism—a place where, thanks to Jean, we could share our ideas with other cat guardians. But the whole unfolding situation put me in a terrible frame of mind.

Hurricane Benny, meanwhile, continued to rage, with his litter box problems, his bullying problems, all his other problems. The odd and yet great part of all this was that I started to use his energy in a positive way. With every leak that sprung from the dam, it became easier and easier for me to emotionally detach and see the issue as just that: a puzzle to solve. This apartment, this fortress of solitude, and the unreal rebellion by Benny became a chance to learn. And I'd be damned if I looked this gift horse in the mouth. It would have been so easy for me to keep "Goddamn, Benny is the most impossible cat to deal with" on a repeating loop in my head, but that, too, was addict behavior. It was a chance to victimize myself, to chalk it up to the universe's desire to shit on me. Recovery taught me that I was able to turn that energy around and say, "Okay, Benny likes routine. He likes stability, he likes sameness. He thrives on those things."

Whenever Benny got into a fur-pulling place, for example, he ended up looking like a poodle, his back end and part of his flank spotty like a lawn overmanicured and burned with fertilizer. I'd be sitting there watching TV and out of the corner of my eye I'd see that jerky head movement, and I'd look up and see him with a mouth full of hair, trying in vain to push it out with his tongue.

I drove myself crazy trying to understand what was going on with Benny, because I kept looking for that one unifying principle that I just *knew* lay behind his issues, the control switch that my inner addict desperately needed to find. There wasn't one, but I couldn't see it because, in order not to go from zero to red in an instant whenever I saw that mouth full of gray-and-white fluff, I was relying on science instead of empathy—working from the neck up instead of from the neck down, which, I know now, will always lead me to a dead end. It is so limiting, because as I was trying to unify, to take the one symptom and give it one root, the cause of the fur pulling was different almost every time. A food allergy, an environmental allergy, shedding his coat for the spring and fall, stress—stress over what? God, it was Benny; it could be stress over Velouria chewing her dinner differently than she did yesterday—sometimes a combination of any or all of the above. Just when I thought I at least had it isolated to certain times of the year, he poodled himself in the middle of July. It wasn't about to be spring or fall, it couldn't be a food allergy, because he was on a special

When What They're Eating Is What's Eating Them

Many animals suffer from undiagnosed allergies their entire lives—many are even allergic to the most common ingredients in pet food, i.e., chicken, fish, corn, beef, and wheat, to name a few. While allergies can be difficult to diagnose, if your animal develops rashes around the face, hotspots, or diarrhea, or starts licking excessively, it's important to work with your vet and rule out food allergies through an eight-week food trial, using a novel protein like venison or rabbit as a nutritional baseline. Environmental allergies are also pervasive, and require more specialized veterinary assistance to diagnose.

Holistic remedies for allergies include natural anti-inflammatories like slippery elm and skin-healing supplements like fish oil. If the route you want to take with your cat in terms of its health is a more holistic one, find a holistic vet in your area by going to www.ahvma.org.

diet, it wasn't cold so it couldn't be stress because of his broken pelvis; it didn't conform to any of the things that I had thought of before.

Then I noticed that he had started keeping vigil, walking back and forth in front of my air conditioner, and finally jumping on top of it. He basically formed a fur-bearing perimeter of stress; he pulled huge chunks of fur off himself and licked them all together, leaving cat-hair origami pieces arranged on the floor around the air conditioner in a huge rectangle. The final piece of the puzzle fell into place when it got hot enough for me to turn on the air conditioner, at which point the smell of piss instantly filled the living room. I took my black light outside and, sure enough, there were cat piss stains all over the outside of the air conditioner—and I mean *all over*—dripping down off the vent, onto the wall beneath, and finally pooling on the ground.

So I began opening the shades, which I usually kept closed. Later that day two totally unfamiliar cats jump up on the air conditioner and . . . just sit there, as if knowing their presence would end in a fun show. When Benny jumped up on the other side of the air conditioner, the teams, separated only by glass now without the addition of the shade, began going *berserk*, and I knew I had my answer. Benny had been killing two birds with one stone, so to speak, relieving the anxiety through pulling and also leaving a visual (and scent-filled) marker with the fur perimeter.

Most other cats would have fought fire with fire, spraying the walls and window on our side of the AC, establishing the "line in the sand," but, naturally, not him. He marked terri-

 Threats from Within Versus Threats from Without

When dealing with territorial insecurity that manifests as inappropriate marking, pay attention to two things:

1. Threats from within. Is the cat competing with other cats, dogs, or children for important resources or socially significant spaces?

2. Threats from without. Are there community cats wandering outside your house that your cats can see through a window or smell from under a door? Their presence will induce what I call the "Alamo response," and your cat will defend his territory by whatever means necessary. If he can't go outside and beat the cats up, he'll pee on the door or below the windows.

tory with his own fur. Benny had shown me yet again that there is no cookie-cutter when it comes to cat behavior.

I used various enzymatic cleaners to clean the living hell out of that wall and got a remote-control-operated air blaster; every time the cats walked up they got shown that the grass was definitely greener elsewhere. My neighbors got blasted quite a few times, too, but since their cats were also being hassled by the strays they forgave me. The offending cats moved on in two days, and Benny stopped pulling his hair out . . . for a few months.

But my challenges were far from over. Because, though I was going to my meetings and working my program, I was still lying to myself on the deepest level. Drugs were still controlling my life. I could pretend that they weren't, because they were prescription drugs, not street drugs, but what it all boiled down to was that I was still a junkie.

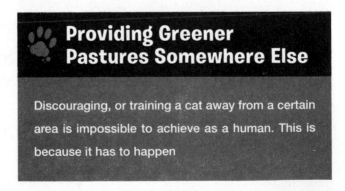

Providing Greener Pastures Somewhere Else

Discouraging, or training a cat away from a certain area is impossible to achieve as a human. This is because it has to happen

1. within two seconds
2. with consistent intensity
3. every single time they come within the forbidden perimeter

If you're at work, you can't spray the cat with water when she jumps on the counter. Do yourself a favor and get a remote training device! You won't need it for more than a few weeks. For instance, one such device is a compressed air canister with an electric eye. The cat jumps up on the counter, the can sprays a spurt of air. The cat jumps down. She won't have to do this too many days in a row before she just decides that the counter is unfriendly. That being said, don't forget my rule of thumb when discouraging a cat from doing something: Behind every "No" there needs to be a "Yes!" If your cats are insistent about the counter, use your cat mojo and figure out *why* it's so important. Then, give them a perch right nearby that's acceptable to you and achieves the important objective for them.

Surrender and
the Falling Scales

think the only way I can explain the way Klonopin bur-
rowed into my fabric is to start by telling the story of the
breakdown I had six months after moving to Boulder with
my girlfriend.

As per my focused career plan, I had started playing gigs
almost immediately after getting to Boulder. I was lucky
enough to get regular shows at a few clubs, which allowed
me to develop a following quickly. Socially it was a perfect
storm—moving to a new place and finding a bunch of people
who loved my music and consequently wanted to party with
me. I fell in with all sorts of different people, most of whom
have faded into the smoke.

And then there was Dan, who worked with me at a coffee shop. He just showed up, having decided to relocate
from LA for no reason. Red flag number one. His dad, Dan

explained, was in the music business, and he himself, a bass player, was living off the royalties from a hit song he'd written for some two-hit wonder band; naturally, I was thrilled when he said he wanted to start a band with me. He wanted to record a demo of my songs and get it to his people in LA so they could sign me. Finally the stars were aligning, as I had known they were meant to from the first time I put a record on that magical old Motorola.

We started working on the demo constantly; as soon as I got off work, Dan and I would go into the studio (my bedroom) with my crappy little four-track cassette recorder, and very quickly I found out that Dan was a terrible bass player and an even worse singer. The only thing Dan was good at, it seemed, was telling me what to do or, as he phrased it, *producing* me. So of course I did what he told me to do, which included playing my own bass as well as every other damn thing on the demo. And the tweaking went on for *months*.

Finally one day he called the coffee shop in the middle of the morning rush. Whoever answered the phone seemed exasperated that he wouldn't take no for an answer, ending her exchange with him by throwing the receiver in the metal sink.

"Guess what?" he said.

"Dude, I'm getting the stink eye from twenty people right now. What is it?"

"My guys in LA called, they love the demo, they want more!"

And I started—this is so embarrassing—running around the coffee shop singing the theme to *The Jeffersons*. You know, "Movin' on up . . ."

So we began work on another demo. The first one, three songs, had taken almost as many months to complete, as I programmed drum machines painstakingly and played the rest of the parts over and over again until I got them right. I wasn't exactly savoring a repeat, but I was blindly following the lead of someone who knew what it was going to take. We started recording again.

And all along, without my realizing it, Dan was, little by little, devouring my entire life. Too little to notice at first— he was like a slow-motion vampire. It's too simple to say that Dan was on the grift; he had *talent*. It seemed like everyone he met, especially females, wound up literally and figuratively screwed. It's not like he was some kind of sculpted Adonis; he was handsome but a lout, his loud, messy, shirts always riding up to expose his gut on one side and his ass crack on the other. But he sold ice to the Eskimos. He convinced girls that he was Valentino; Christ, he convinced me that he was a musician. The core of his brilliance, like the best con men, was unshakable confidence and skills of manipulation. He was an absolutely astonishing liar. I've never met—and I hope never to meet again—anyone else who could flat-out lie, eyeball to eyeball, like him. It was amazing, except I thought somehow I was immune to it. I guess so did everyone else.

In short order he had moved in with me and my girlfriend—brilliant idea, right?—and was seducing her, or at least it seemed that way to me. I figured how could you fight like that without having the same passion on the flip side? The tireless Dan was also busy seducing our drummer and fucking her up to the point that she was showing up drunk as hell just to get through rehearsals. He was a walking id, a dick-shaped time bomb, and eventually he went off. Screaming matches with whoever was in earshot. Punched-out holes in the wall. Busted-out windows, calls from neighbors, and being dragged away in handcuffs. The energy of rage scared the hell out of me (as it always has—energy that goes floor to ceiling makes me want to hide; where do you think I developed the skills to "whisper" to new cats?). So I alternately defused the bomb (by placating Dan) and just stayed away. I got home from work and left immediately to play guitar on the street, leaving him and my girlfriend to hate or love on each other, which in my increasingly paranoid state I believed could only happen if they were also screwing.

I could feel myself losing it. I was in therapy, I was trying to get hold of what was slipping away from me, but it was like trying to take hold of water. The harder you grip your sanity, the faster it runs out of your hands. The end came when I needed to go to Dan's room to get something and found pages and pages covered in my forged signature. I started looking into things more and realized that not only had he been stealing money from me—not that I had much—running up phone and cable bills with porn in the middle of the night, signing my name to thousands of dollars' worth of checks, but also that all his stories about his father and the demo and his people in LA had been complete fabrications. I confronted him, had the conversation I had rehearsed endlessly with my therapist, and told him to get out of town or I would have him arrested. By the next morning he was gone.

But I was through. That last act, instead of giving me relief, just flooded my psychic engine completely. I couldn't be of use to anybody. I couldn't work. I couldn't make music. I couldn't have human relationships anymore. I was just finished.

Even today, this is almost embarrassing to write about. Oh, this guy came into my life, caused some chaos, and I'm going to blame him for the fact that I went crazy. But that's not what was going on. He simply exposed an enormous flaw. I lived like a child, I trusted like a child. I was a lifelong artist who looked to be enveloped by others' caring because I had absolutely no life skills. I'm not talking about typing or filing. I had never developed a way to *cope* with anything. My house was not the straw one blown in by the big, bad wolf;

mine was made of tissue, torn apart by the breeze of a few harshly spoken words, and as Dan ran out of Boulder, back to the safety of LA or wherever the hell he actually came from, the only thing that happened was that I could finally breathe enough to have a complete nervous breakdown.

"Please," I begged my psychiatrist. "Just hospitalize me."

"Jackson," she said soothingly, "you don't need to be hospitalized. I think you're just suffering from some real anxiety."

"No, you don't get it. I am going *insane*. Put me away. A seventy-two-hour vacation."

"I'm going to write you a prescription for Klonopin, which is an antianxiety medication," she said, handing me a piece of paper. "Don't take it unless you absolutely need to. But you're going to be fine." And then she eyed the door—my hint to get the hell out.

Don't take it unless I absolutely need to. Right. No amount of the substances with which I normally medicated myself could put a dent in the anxiety and the depression, so during my lunch break at the coffee place I called my girlfriend and insisted she bring the pill to me at work, because I couldn't stand it one more minute and at the same time I didn't have enough money to stagger off into the sunset. I had to get through these days. She came over and we sat outside on a bench while waiting for it to take effect. Much of the next ten years is in-and-out, but the next forty-five minutes after taking that first pill remain my clearest memory until detoxing. She watched me intently, worried about the wind kicking up around my mental card house. At the forty-minute mark it hit me. Like the wet hallucinogen dreams but with no edge at all. My mouth fell open wide enough for the magic carpet to fly out. This wash came over me, this knee-knocking, slow-motion, warm tidal wave. It started at the knees and went to the groin, this beautiful buzz, and rose from there, until the final place it hit was my mouth. (Later on, everyone would know when I was buzzing—practically ODing—on Klonopin, because my slur was really bad. To this day I know when people are on medications like Klonopin or Xanax or other benzodiazepines, because the dry mouth and the slurring are just dead giveaways.)

I remember looking up after the initial nod, what must've been a few minutes later, and seeing my girlfriend crying. And I remember, mercifully, not caring. Years later I asked her why she had started crying that day and she said that, in that moment, she knew she had lost me for good.

She was right. In the few months that followed, I completely pushed her away. When I was pilled, I experienced everything at a distance. Emotions like love and loss were, in my state, matches burning under a house of cards. I had to protect the house and that meant extinguishing the fire. My girlfriend and I had been through so much—she had fought for me harder than anyone ever had, and within a few months, she was gone. And I don't remember her leaving.

But I was OK with that, because my finger was finally removed from the ungrounded outlet and the shock was replaced with gentle waves. I had finally solved my oversensitivity problem. Klonopin was the essence of going away. And for the next ten years, this was the one thing I could rely on. Weed, coke, booze, acid, mushrooms—those things could be good or bad on any given day. But with Klonopin, I always knew exactly what was going to happen. And, just as important, *when* it would happen. Forty minutes. No matter what degree of teeth-grinding, death-spiraling, send-me-to-a-dark-corner-gripping-my-knees-and-rocking-back-and-forth hell I was going through, I knew I could hang on for another forty minutes. And it was legal, and I got it from a doctor.

So on that day, ten years later, when Dmitri, the fast-talking lawyer, and his friends had come over to my house to get rid of my stash, it seemed perfectly reasonable not to tell them about the Klonopin I had hidden in plain sight in other prescription bottles, in the nightstand, in three different decorative pocket pill holders, under the sink next to the toilet paper. After all, Klonopin wasn't drugs, I reasoned; it was *medicine*.

Maybe this attitude was the reason my twelve-step sponsors kept firing me.

My first sponsor was a young guy who seemed to be *every-body's* sponsor. He had a sense of humor, he had a wife and a kid, he had stability, he had a good head on his shoulders. And maybe that's why he was the grand pooh-bah of Boulder sponsors: you pick a sponsor who has what you want, and he had a lot—he was a young grownup.

We met three or four times, and he kept getting hung up on Klonopin. We glanced over the first few steps, but finally one day, over coffee, he just stopped and said, "We can't go any further until you clean up."

Not this again. "Tony, I *am* clean. How many times do I have to tell you before you believe me? I don't smoke pot, drink, snort coke, take hallucinogens, drink cough syrup, I don't do any of that stuff anymore."

"Yeah, but you still abuse prescription drugs."

"No, actually, I *don't*. I take what I'm *supposed* to take. What is *prescribed* to me." I didn't mention that it was prescribed to me by two different doctors, neither of whom knew about the other.

"I'm sorry, Jackson. You're not clean. Find another sponsor."

And that hurt, and if it hadn't been for the fact that I was going out with Jen, I probably would have quit. But I wanted her to approve of my recovery. She wanted me to have a sponsor, so I met with another potential one. And I don't even remember his name, because we only met once, and he said, "Come back when you're off Klonopin."

Meanwhile my friends in recovery—especially my friend Karl, who would ultimately become my sponsor, guiding me and keeping me level through every peak and valley since then—all of them were raking me over the coals. They said if I wanted to be clean and sober, not just *dry*, I had to lead a life of unflinching honesty. So finally, just to shut them all up and show them they were wrong, I went to the doctor and explained what was really going on.

He had an office very clearly designed to project the fruits of his labor. It was very, very fruitful. He had a massive gently flowing water wall behind him, and the first thing he said, leaning over his desk, separating from his reflective watery background as if he were about to tell me where the Holy Grail was hiding, was, "You're taking enough Klonopin to kill a rhino." I couldn't just stop, he explained, because I would have seizures and die; I needed to step down slowly, but I had to do it *immediately*.

I admitted to the doc that for most of the time he had been treating me I had also been an alcoholic and a hopeless dope fiend. Dignified but disgusted, he told me he wasn't going to sit around and watch me die. He would oversee the step-down, he said; he knew my other doctor and called her to say she couldn't refill my scrip. The jig was up. His reaction was the mirror I needed to look into, the wall to fall back against. The only thing that has ever saved me in this life has been the walls that I have been backed into. This time it just happened to be watery and backlit.

I brought the news back to my recovery allies, especially Karl and Jen (who couldn't stand one another but rallied around me from opposite sides), and their support was unflagging.

And thank God for that, because getting clean from Klonopin would be like, in Karl's words of warning, pulling a rebar out of my ass one inch at a time. Every time I stepped down over the next three months, it just fucking hurt, physically and mentally, and in the last three days the pain was unbearable.

As the step-down came to a close I was going to meetings constantly—the last seventy-two hours before the last pill and the seventy-two hours after were simply the worst days of my life. The pain of withdrawal was bigger than the crazy I had tried to escape ten years prior. The emotions behind the imbalance were just off in a corner, just past my peripheral vision, getting bigger every day. So when I lost access to the "off" switch, the gentle tidal wave turned into a gigantic cold washing machine and kicked the shit out of me. I wanted to be dead. The first twelve hours after Klonopin, I would puke, drink tea, and Jen would put a washcloth on my head and say things like "this too shall pass," but I didn't think it ever would. Suddenly my synapses would begin to fire again and I would hallucinate all kinds of waking nightmares. And then I would puke again.

For weeks afterward I needed to be driven to and from places after dark because of the tracers I was still seeing, the photosensitivity. My sponsors were right. At Karl's nagging, I reset my clean date, wiping out six months of what I had thought was sobriety, as I began to climb the biggest hill I would ever encounter.

It was in this state—raw, tender, newly hatched—that I went back to New York three months later to visit my family. My relationship with my parents had deteriorated over the course of my addiction—and the closer to ninety days of *true sobriety* I got, the closer to the surface my emotions toward them swam, the more irrepressible they became, until I couldn't tolerate even being near my parents. These new emotions felt like teenage rebellion times forty. They pierced any wall you tried to erect as if it were made of applesauce. It sounds awful but it's true—the gift of recovery is that you *get* to experience those fucked-up feelings. I got to feel that things I saw in my parents were in me, too. I was a continuation of them. In this extended moment, that realization affected me constantly, as if I were sewn into the itchiest sweater on earth; I hated the parts of us that were exactly the same. I could no longer play the wronged one; the three of us were all perpetrator and victim alike. I just wanted a simple target at which to point that easiest of emotions, rage. Instead, my confusion made me hate them, myself, the whole world—and that feeling was simply intolerable.

So I was out to lunch with my cousin one day, swimming in the deep end of these complex, fucked-up feelings, and I found myself screaming. They need to do this, they need to do that, they need to be more of this, they need not to be so much that.

And my cousin looked at me and said, very innocently, "Jackson, what do you expect from them? They're in their seventies. Do you really want to change them?"

"Of *course* I want to change them!" I said loudly enough that we both looked around to see if I was going to get kicked out of the diner. And as soon as the words came out of my mouth I realized how ridiculous they were. There was nothing I could do to change them. I was powerless over them.

Any time you prove to an addict that he can't control the universe, it's a massive blow. I went almost immediately from being full of rage to being equally full of sadness. I started a decline into depression. A week later, on a hot, muggy, disgusting New York summer day, I went to my brother's place, because I couldn't stand being at my parents' for one more minute, and being there made things even worse, because my brother was in amazing shape. I didn't exactly want his life, but he had all these things that I knew I was forever removed from, a dream reserved for lighter sheep than I. A great job. A terrific wife who was about to give birth. *Stability*.

Feeling like I was watching them from the wrong side of a TV, I felt paranoid. Judged. I left to go back to my parents' apartment, and as I walked toward the bus stop, that removed vibe just grew until it swallowed me; I felt so far outside of the experience of the people who were walking past me that I couldn't even imagine what it must be like to live a normal life.

And when I got to the bus stop, desperate to hunker down into myself for the twenty-block ride to my parents' place and then just to hibernate there, I realized I didn't have bus fare.

And then it started raining.

It wasn't enough that my parents had had their fingers on my buttons for years. It wasn't enough that my brother and his perfect life were right in front of me to show me how deeply I had screwed everything up. Now God was laughing at me. (As an addict I take everything as a sign from God. It was pouring on about eight million people but I was the only one getting wet.)

I started talking out loud. In all of my years as a drug addict I never talked out loud to myself, but when I got sober I started. "What do you want from me?" I said, to the universe I guess. "What am I supposed to do?" And it wasn't God, it was the voice of my sponsor and everyone who had been fed up with me saying, "Surrender. Hit your knees, you egomaniacal son of a bitch. Surrender to victory."

In a truly desperate attempt not to rip off my clothes and run through the streets screaming until a merciful cop picked me up and gave me seventy-two equally merciful hours in Bellevue, I went through my meager twelve-step toolbox, reciting and responding: The first of the twelve steps is, "We admitted we were powerless over drugs and alcohol—that our lives had become unmanageable." Right; done. I was unmanageability personified. The second, "We came to believe that a power greater than ourselves could restore us to sanity." Well, of course. This much we know . . . at this point I'd seen everything through the warped sunglasses of the lower power, so obviously the higher had to be a smarter choice, right? And the third, "We made a decision to turn our will and our lives over to the care of God as we understood him." This was that moment. Showtime, asshole. What could I lose? I had literally tried every other way. I was so tired. So *tired*.

I turned my will and my life over to the universe.

I hit my knees on the corner of 98th and Broadway and looked up, seriously straining to see the universe through the light-reflected purple muck of the raining Manhattan sky. I didn't know what the hell I was doing. I had never prayed in my life. I mean, I had prayed for *stuff*—I had prayed for sex, I had prayed for drugs, I had prayed for a record contract. Foxhole prayers are easy. Bargaining with the Almighty for an easy way out of a very messy situation. "Please, God, I'm about to get my balls blown off, if you rescue me I'll become a rabbi." But this was decidedly different . . . difficult. I didn't *want anything*. I wanted to cry. It had been a while. I wanted to stop being angry. I wanted for this rain to make me clean. I wanted to throw my body into the maternal arms of the universe and have her rock me to sleep.

Whenever I would overintellectualize recovery, so as not to feel it—from the neck up offered an easier, more familiar out than from the neck down—Karl would tell me, an eye roll not so hidden in his voice, "Jackson, just hit your knees first thing in the morning and last thing at night. You don't have to pray, really, just do the action. Act as if you are humbled and grateful not to be the master of the universe." And I did it. I gave up.

I surrendered.

I would love to say this was the only moment in my life I had to drop to my knees—the only instance in my life that I pushed myself to the brink and then had to surrender again, but I've done it so many times I can't even count. In nine years I've grabbed that steering wheel back and had to let it go again once a day, sometimes ten times a day, sometimes I go a couple of months without doing it. But I surrender every time, because now I know that it feels *good* to admit that I can't control the universe.

When I got back to Boulder, deep in the heart of the vulnerable and the surrendered, observations seemed to become invested with more than detached, "scientific" curiosity. I suddenly felt what I saw.

It's 7:00 p.m. in early November. I've always been very sensitive to the turning back of the clocks. Early darkness screws me up 100 percent. Now, I love seasons, I love the Colorado winter. But the darkness, man, I'm going to have to fight that sonofabitch for the next four months. I'm not complaining: four consults in a single day feels like I'm on the verge of having an actual job. But I'm so bone-dragging tired. Absolutely nothing about today's consults was automatic. One after the other where I really had to look for universal guidance, as well as guidance from the cats themselves. Dropping my bag at the door, I fall into some kind of waking, standing coma. Benny walks in, in full "I'm a cat?" bus driver mode. And just like it happened a few weeks ago, after all the overthinking and deflecting, I find myself on my knees in the rain again. Benny has changed.

Or am I changing?

Stay with it, Galaxy, don't think your way out of this particular paper bag. Just let it go. . . .

I'm so afraid to blink, I'm tearing up. The TV, mindlessly babbling since I always leave it on for the cats, tries to distract me. Just disinvite it to the party . . . tune it out . . . I am so afraid to move, afraid this dream will end and drift off into the slate chill of outside. I'm moving but not moving. I see him completely and feel that he sees me. Without the hallucinogens I thought had been providing me with some extraterrestrial insight for all these years, I can do the bullet-dodging, slow-motion dance of human and bullets in *The Matrix*. Benny is not just a cat who I take care of but a confused, frustrated being who is exactly the same as me. This is the flipside of the same avalanche I just lived through with my parents, I resisted then, as now, the things that made us the same. Now there were just two misfits staring at each other in a funhouse mirror. Resentment doesn't work. Rage has no seat at the table. Even confusion steps out for a cigarette.

And the scales fall from my eyes.

Benny and I are both socially isolated, behaviorally unlubricated, two fingers on the same hand caught in the massive gears. This is what differentiates sympathy from empathy. No matter how much I care for you, it's not until I recognize me in you and you in me that the veil of gauze is lifted on the world.

I hit my knees. And then I'm on my ass. The cheap floor of my apartment shakes and Benny's ears turn 180 degrees away from me. The shame rushes in as the dream rushes out; I can't believe how selfishly I've been seeing him, how I've been holding him to human standards, standards that are neither higher nor lower than cat standards but completely irrelevant. Now that my brain is finally free from all the shit I was drowning it in, I see, in the shock of a new connection, how little I've truly understood him, and I am filled with horror and shame. All of the time I've laughingly dismissed his "bus driver who fell asleep and woke up a cat" looks—he's shared my life for years and just *now* I realize the deep level of his frustration and resulting anxiety?

It would be awfully poetic if I could say I cried like a baby when I saw him walk into the living room at that moment, bus driver to cat. But sobbing, losing myself in the release of sadness, was something that wouldn't come back to me easily for years. Nevertheless, I misted up and asked him to come to me. It's a pointless exercise to ask a cat for forgiveness. You do what you do when they do what they do—move on. They scratch the couch, they piss on the carpet? You have no choice—move on. You feel sorrow and shame for the dismissive and overly simplified shapes that you've imposed on the animals you revere? No choice. . . . Not that this stopped me. As much as he hated it, I held him tightly. *This is one last moment just for me, bud*, I thought. *The rest will be yours.*

At that moment, once again, I started over. There was no space left for embarrassment, just rediscovery and reinvention. I began to approach him as the cat he was, not as a differently shaped human, and he responded. In the days that followed, I took it back to the start and simply followed him. I watched every tic, put it in the context of this new being that I felt I had just met, building for him a story that matched his outside. It was just like it had been when I was studying acting—I asked questions: What is the inner life of this cat? What happened in the moments before and after he makes contact with me? Where is he going? What has he left? Why does he lead with his chest and why does he slump his shoulders?

Once again, from all the clues I gathered, I made up a workable story, one that I could re-create in myself. I settled on a being, a character out of an Oliver Sacks book, who, every time he woke up, had to be reassured who he was, that he belonged, and that he knew how to the operate the complex machinery that made up a cat. I did this through my communications with Benny as well as adjusting his physical environment—even more than before, "sameness" was the order of the day. And then he needed to figure out how to claim and settle into his territory from day to day. I used one specific treat that he enjoyed to guide him from socially significant spot to spot. We did it the same way every day. Each meal would be placed identically; I would scoop boxes and keep the same amount of litter. This ritualistic stability included his relationship with me and Velouria. I would invite him up to the bed at night to displace Velouria. I felt it was good for both of them, to have a time-sharing arrangement revolving around the territorial throne, the bed. I just had to keep reminding him every night that come twenty minutes after lights out, after she had chest time with me, he could come around and claim it. She would take up residence at the far end of the king-size bed, and another day of retraining a cat amnesiac would come to a close.

Believe it or not, this complicated-sounding routine was suddenly second nature to me. Given the merciful space and time that my new apartment/laboratory presented, my observational skills became just that much sharper. Just as the early experiments with Cat, I Love You proved to be sort of a Rosetta Stone into the inner world of cats, Benny brought that sense of discovery to life. Everything I tried on him and Velouria, I brought back to the cats I worked with. I found a world of similarities, and just as important, a new stillness inside me—I could breathe through the process, and just wait for each cat's next move.With Benny, I just had to give his behaviors a context that worked for me, a picture my actor self could inhabit or my artist self could paint, and we were off to the races. And the more I did this, the more I was able to work with all cats, not just him, on their level and not on mine. This is what I do when I work with your cat today. I gather clues to create a life story; then I give you that story infused with the lessons of Cat Mojo 101 so you can understand your cat's behavior from *her* perspective instead of yours. That's when bonds deepen and problems are given the space to untangle.

This was what my brain and emotions coming back to life allowed me to do—I could be present in the moment for an animal who needed me to be present in the moment.

The problem is that addicts have a mortal fear of being present in the moment.

Forgive and Move On

Cats have a short-term attention span of less than three seconds. This in itself makes the concept of discipline a farce. Here's how to deal with troublesome behavior:

- In the moment: Count to ten, clean up, forgive and move on. Anything else you do right now will erode the bond between you and your cat.
- Moving forward: Develop a long-term behavioral action plan informed by past moments of transgression.

Everything
Still Tastes
Like More

There's an unfortunate glamour to alcoholism, to drug addiction: whether it's James Dean flying off a cliff, Kurt Cobain blowing his face off, tales of glorious excess from the likes of John Bonham and Keith Moon, these things are all—what—attractive? Somehow we see glamour in the last drooling, incoherent days of our idols.

There is, however, no glamour in being Mama Cass, Orson Welles, or Marlon Brando. Food addiction is not glamorous; it's just humiliating. And yet for so many of us it's the primal addiction. At six years old I couldn't smoke or drink. But I could hoard and sneak food, and it was the buzz I got from doing that that I recognized in later years from pot, alcohol, pills. After all of the things I've talked about in terms of recognizing who I am, going to my first meeting, seeing myself in other drug addicts, other alcoholics, other smokers, other compulsive human beings, it was still a long painful road from there toward uncovering the primal from the swamp of shame that lay on top of it. I am an addict: An alcoholic. A drug addict. A food addict. The first two are easy now to say. The third isn't and maybe it never will be. It makes me cringe.

When I moved out of the apartment I had shared with Beth, it was the first time in my life I got to live by myself. I thought it would be an instant feeling of freedom, but all it turned out to be was an opportunity to isolate myself. Any of "us" know that this is an invitation for our addict to come out and play. I'd broken up with girlfriends, broken up with my band, broken up with my friends, I wasn't working at the shelter anymore, I was working on my own, my office was in my apartment. There were times when I didn't shower or leave my apartment for four or five days. I was a "dry drunk," not using but not working a program either; I was Caligula looking for a fix.

I wasn't indulging in dope or drink or pills anymore, but I had to continue to "fill the void," and finally this subconscious mission became literal. "Suddenly," I was seeking out and living off of unbelievable quantities of fast food. I would have actual food blackouts; finding myself driving out of a fast-food place not knowing how I got in. I made light of it—it became part of my fat-guy repertoire. But let's break it down. A double Whopper with cheese has 1,061 calories and 68 grams of fat, and for lunch I would eat two of them, plus a chicken sandwich (750 cal/45 g fat), plus a shake (760 cal/ 24 g fat), and a couple orders of fries (500 cal each/24 g fat). That's 4,632 calories /253 grams of fat, for all of you count-ing. Which I never, till this moment, did.

Then I'd do the same thing somewhere else for dinner.

All my mirrors showed me from the neck up. You can't blame me for not wanting to see anything else. But at one point my apartment building was being fumigated and I had to relocate for a few days. I took the cats over to Kate's while she and her husband were out of town; to help keep them grounded in their routine while their territory was upside down, I kept them playing as much as possible. Benny was a play voyeur. He seemed to gather calm by watching Velouria absolutely go bananas. I was, as always, nicely outside of my own body while paying attention to them both, acting as Velouria's surrogate prey as she did me proud by just being herself, a consistently amazing lit-tle hunter and jumper, while Benny gazed on, inscrutable. I trailed her fishing pole toy across the hard stone of the office, and UP! she flipped like a ballerina and caught the feather in midair. I was doing this play at first mov-ing around the basement, but I ran out of breath, so I sat in an office chair, praising Velouria as Benny watched her snag her feathery prey and run off, clanking the pole behind her.

And then I caught a glance of something. The office itself was lit with desk lamps, and there were glass French doors separating the office from the rest of the basement, which was completely dark. Those doors had closed, and the reflection of the lamps created a ghosted mirror of Benny and me. And seeing it, I recognized only one of us.

Looking at myself, I thought, "Who are you?" All of the years that I vainly struggled to retain identification, ownership of this mortal coil. And in the end, I don't even know whose body this is.

In the blink of an eye, my emotions bungeed from the bridge, the gorge spinning around me, the rocks approaching rapidly. The depression was sudden, a punch to the eye from a brass-knuckled hairy fist. Then, bobbing and weaving from the onslaught, I went straight to, "You know what? Fuck it. I'm done." I was speaking to food. "I'm finished. I'm not dieting anymore. I lose ninety, I gain one hundred and twenty and I am losing this fight and I will always lose this fight, so if you want to be the thing that takes me, then fucking take me, I don't care anymore. Are you proud of yourself? Well before you gloat, remember this: You get to kill me but I'm already dead."

And over the next nine months I gained another eighty-five pounds, weighing in finally at four hundred pounds.

. . .

Jean and I, meanwhile, had been through a lot. But two people can live in the same pair of pants for only so long. As anyone who has had a business partner can attest, it felt like we might as well have been sleeping together. We spent way too much time together. Every decision made by two brains, every dollar spent. Our vision for the products and for our ideology never diverged. I was, however, building resentments during the time of her recovery from her heart condition; I was convinced that at the end of the day, she just wasn't pulling her weight. I would sit at my desk, falling asleep in front of a thrice-revised mission statement, knowing that Jean had been asleep for hours, and I would start that seemingly unstoppable argument that I was only able to accomplish in my thoughts. There is an inherent problem with this kind of karmic constipation—flower essences *are* an energetic medicine, and if you're sitting there thinking poisonous thoughts while you make them, it will just be passed on, a vibrational bad penny. So I knew that the problem really had to be solved.

One day I came home from doing a consult and when I petted Benny, he backed away out of arm's reach with a decidedly funny look, both facially and physically. And within thirty seconds he started to throw up. Then something took a radically weird turn and he started to hurl himself against the wall, foam flying out of his mouth. I had never seen any-thing like it in my life.

I got in my car—all four hundred pounds of me—and went screeching with him over to the twenty-four-hour clinic, and meanwhile the foam was just pouring out of him, covering the outside of his soft-sided carrier. I was consumed with panic, but had to keep talking to him, keeping one hand on him. They got him on the table, and immediately he started dying.

"What the hell is happening?" said the vet, both to me and her tech simultaneously.

"I don't know," I said.

"I don't know!!" yelled the tech, trying to intubate Benny and failing. His convulsions were simply heartbreaking—and worse, baffling to the professionals in front of me.

"I mean, he had a dental done a couple weeks ago," I stuttered, "and he had a hard time coming out of anesthesia. Like, it took way too long. He wasn't right for days."

"That's what it is, then," the vet said. "That was demon-strating an underlying heart condition, and this has to be a heart attack."

And then Benny died.

The vet brought him back with an epinephrine shot, but immediately he started foaming up again.

I remember, in that moment of unbridled panic and des-peration, asking him, *Do you want me to let you go?* And his convulsions stopped and he stared me dead in the eye. I knew—I don't know how I knew, but I *knew*—that he was telling me he wasn't ready. The vet was asking me to let him go. So was the tech. And I said, "No—keep working."

The vet thought I was insane, but we fought for Benny's life for hours. She kept telling me, "You might want to say good-bye." Finally, when he died *again* on the table and we brought him back *again*, when he was resting for a moment in an oxygen chamber, I collapsed outside around a cigarette. And after six hours of the worst kind of bad trip, the idea occurred to me to ask for help.

Don't get me wrong—there were many people to call. Friends, sober friends, my sponsor, bandmates, old HSBV coworkers, all of the vets I had made connections with in my first few years of consulting. I just didn't think of being anything but alone. Again, as always, this was classic addict behavior. Addiction is incredibly isolating. Inevitably there's a bridge crossed where *partying* with others becomes *procuring, preparing,* and *using*—alone. You spend all your time getting high by yourself and doing all those rituals by yourself, and then later, when you're clean and all these feelings are woken up, and you're starting to live again and experience emotion again, there's something in you that says, well, you should be doing that by yourself, too. Demonstrating *anything* was shameful. I was off Klonopin. Jen, in a multiprescription-drug-fueled haze, had broken up with me, and I thought I was alone. That was no reason in itself to panic. I just was.

But as the slowest-burning cartoon lightbulb imaginable ignited above my head, I realized that I could call Jean. I didn't want to, because I wanted to keep my relationship with her at that point very strictly business, since I knew our partnership was on the brink, but at that moment I thought, *I'm lost without her and I don't know what to do and I need her.* So I called her, and somehow, driving down from 10,000 feet, she was there in fifteen minutes.

And *then* things got crazy.

Jean walked into the room, looked at Benny, and said to me, before she even put her bag down, "I don't think that's a heart condition. I think he's choking on something." And the more she talked, the more it made sense.

"Absolutely not," said the vet.

"Can't you just X-ray him to check?" I said.

"With his heart condition, because that's what this obviously is, the stress of putting him under the X-ray would kill him." And nothing Jean or I could say would change her mind.

But finally her shift was over, and when her replacement

came in to relieve her, he took one look at Benny and said, "I don't know what this is, it may be a heart condition, he may be choking, but he's dying either way, so we might as well at least find out whether there might be a way to save him."

So we got to the X-ray and, sure enough, there was some kind of blockage. Benny was not a big cat (he always hovered around seven pounds), and I looked at the X-ray and said, incredulous and somehow relieved that there was an answer, "Is that a *Matchbox car*?" It was as if he'd swallowed something not a whole lot smaller than he was.

"Whatever it is," said Jean, "the damn thing has to come *out*."

"We don't have an endoscope," the relief vet said gently. Our only choice, she said, was to go to another animal hospital, twenty-five miles away, wake up the surgeon—it was 1:00 a.m. by now—scope Benny, and figure out what the hell was going on.

The problem was, Benny was so freaked out that, if he got in the backseat of my car awake, he was going to give himself that heart attack that the first vet had practically wished into existence. So we had to sedate him. But we couldn't give him anesthesia, because you can't drive around with an open, functioning oxygen tank in the backseat of your piece-of-crap car. So the vet and her tech sedated him with an IV and intubated him, which was pretty amazing—to put a tube down the throat of a cat whose throat is already clogged up—and then Jean got in the backseat of my car with Benny's limp body in one hand, and the airway bag in the other, squeezing it rhythmically, breathing for him, and I got in the front seat and I drove that goddamn car like it was a rocket with the *Dukes of Hazzard* theme song playing, with Jean yelling, "Drive faster! Drive faster!" because on IV sedation he would wake up in about twenty minutes, and that was the one thing that absolutely could not happen. I made the twenty-five miles from Boulder to Wheat Ridge in twelve minutes.

When we got there, Jean went running in—this was where bulldozer Jean worked really well—put Benny on the counter in the bag, and said, "This cat needs to have an endoscopy *right now*."

And the guy at the front desk said, "Well, first we need to—"

"RIGHT NOW!" Jean exploded, and there is not a person on earth who could have disobeyed her.

She got us into the operation room to witness as the surgeon, distinguished and disheveled from the bed we had just pulled him out of, took the scope and slid it in Benny's throat with an incredible agility, and he showed us what was down there: a hair ball.

The biggest fucking hair ball I have ever seen, to this day. I still have a picture. For the price I paid, I should frame it.

Instantly, as he pulled the hair ball out, Benny got his

color back and started breathing again. And then he pulled out another hair ball, and that was that. Benny went into recovery and stayed at the hospital for three days so his insides could get back to normal. The bill was $3,600, and I remember this because that was the day I decided I didn't care if I maxed out my credit cards, because that was how you have to live. And yes, I thought about how many times I had run credit card cons to get drugs, and what I would have done once for $3,600 of dope. Being able to take care of that boy was what guardianship was all about. I felt . . . clean.

And the next day when I talked to Jean, it was with not a sense of resentment but with an incredible depth of appreciation for who she was and everything she had brought to my life, and it changed our relationship on the spot. Being reminded of how much I loved her as an unbelievable presence in my life, and how a few years before she had allowed me to walk out of that shelter and into a new phase of my life absolutely holding my hand, absolutely guiding me through—it also reminded me of what's truly important in life. I didn't care anymore that our business was dissolving. I would make it work for her, and I would make it worth her while to sell me her interest in Spirit Essences and Little Big Cat. And she was totally amenable to it. I would own the company outright, and I wouldn't feel resentment anymore about working constantly for her because I'd be working for me.

The Last Supper
with My
Compulsive Other

By now I was no longer having blackouts at fast-food drive-throughs and joking about them with friends; I was literally drowning in food. I ate 24/7. Yes. I fell asleep chewing. Didn't even think that was possible. Just like when you're trying to make sure that your dope is taken care of, you don't wait until you've got four joints left, you don't wait until you've got three lines of coke left, you don't wait until you've got a quarter bottle of wine left, you don't wait until you've got two cigarettes left—you do not wait until you've got two pieces of leftover pizza in the house. You line up everything so that you can enable your isolation, so that you can make sure that your perceived control over the universe is in place. You're always thinking three steps ahead. I'd buy four orders of large fries so that I could have two right away and two later that night.

I kept getting accidental feedback from others and doing an amazing job of ignoring it.

"What are you doing today?" my mom said once on the phone.

"Well," I said, "I was going to go to the mall, but I can't get my feet in my shoes today."

There was a long pause. "What do you mean, today?"

"Oh, there are just some days when my feet just get big and I can't get them into my shoes, so I walk around barefoot."

"Honey," my mom said very carefully, "that's called edema, and it's your heart. You have to get to the hospital right now."

But going to the hospital would have been a big pain in the ass. So I bargained. "I'll go tomorrow, Mom."

"No," and then in measured tones, "you need to go now."

"It's the weekend, which means I'd have to go to the ER, and I don't have money for that."

"Honey," I heard the unmistakable tone of her speaking through her teeth, "I. Don't. Care."

She just wouldn't let me slither out, so I finally went to the hospital, and sure enough, I had edema. I still have the marks on my legs and feet from how swollen they were, the busted blood vessels that just became part of the scenery.

When I went home to New York, my family never said,

"You're fat." But my dad, who is diabetic, would always be running around the house trying to poke me with his little meter to get my blood sugar level. And I'd make fun of him and say, "Dad, do you realize how old and Jewish this makes you look? Will you stop? I'm fine." He and his glucometer finally caught up with me, hovering over my air mattress at 7:00 a.m. I looked up and he was standing there. Terrified and vaguely surprised I wasn't lying in a puddle, I said, "You know what, fuck it, take my blood."

"Thank you," he said, and poked me with the thing. And when he was done, he looked at it, and all the blood drained from his face, because my glucose was at around 400, which, I found out quickly, is fucking high. He was fighting the twin towers of fear for the life of his son and the desire to say I told you so. This wasn't his usual vicarious hypochondria; I was diabetic.

But I *still* didn't do anything. And the dominoes continued to fall. There is, I believe, a very specific number, and at one pound over that number your body begins to tell you to screw off; it will not work any more overtime to support an uncaring employer. Things just fail.

"I see how big you are," said a friend I'd met while at the vet with Benny, a friend whose husband had sleep apnea, "and I see that look in your eyes from the twenty cups of coffee you have to drink to stay up. You need to have a sleep study done."

I rolled my eyes with the subtext of, "*So* don't have time for that."

"You do realize this could kill you?'

"Yeah," I said, "but I'm *really* busy."

That's actually what I said. "Yeah, but I'm *really* busy."

I did the sleep study despite the protestations of my lower self. And it turned out that I was having sixty episodes an hour in which I held my breath for more than thirty seconds, which meant that for more than thirty minutes per hour I wasn't breathing. And during these episodes, there was no way to get into REM sleep. I was literally not sleeping. I was diagnosed with sleep apnea and introduced to what I called the "mask-and-hose snorkel"—the contraption that hooks you up to the awful CPAP machine—that I had to wear while I slept. Mostly the thing wound up thrown violently on the floor.

My blood pressure was sky high. I had crippling incidents of gout, which kept me either at home or getting around with a walking stick. One night, as I was heading into the supermarket, a jacked-up Jeep came screaming to a halt feet from me and a very pretty stranger, coincidentally in the crosswalk. The Jeep sat, idled, and revved as I "walked" past its headlights; I had two walking sticks because both of my feet were being ravaged and it was almost impossible to get around. "Move a little slower, you fat fuck!" the letter-jacketed high schooler driving the Jeep spat. I limped to my shopping cart and glanced at the stranger, who was looking at me with a mix of disgust and pity. Once upon a time I would have instantly started flirting with her. Now her pretty face was a mirror in which I saw that I was fat, broken, and lonely.

I was the person online dating was invented for, or so it seemed. I got the thrill of seduction without ever getting up from my desk. I spent deliciously long times spinning webs, delighting in the narcotic of fear and desire, explaining to Benny how *this* one was going to be the one. Velouria, I decided, was just beyond caring.

The problem came when I met the women. One after another, the spells were broken unceremoniously. It wasn't enough to be desired by someone, even in my state—want had to be a two-way deal. It was a really awful feeling, going through six weeks of fantastical online gymnastics with women who were willing to meet me in spite of my weight, meeting them, feeling the spell break, and ushering them unceremoniously out of my space (both physically and emotionally), seemingly in an instant, as Benny and Velouria looked on. I just couldn't lie.

Jill was immediately different; I didn't need to puff out my artistic chest, didn't need to flaunt the planks that made up my sociopolitical platform. She couldn't give a damn. She was about the laughter and the want, and those two things started my motor from the deep freeze. Jill and I, from the day we e-met, laughed our asses off. Serious water-shooting-out-your-nose, knee-buckling, snorting fits. I recognized her as family, something I had been missing for so long. I could lay my four hundred pounds bare and I knew she just didn't care. She had a family, friends, a steady job—in other words, things that ruled out stark, raving mad. She ran a dog-walking and pet-sitting business in Redondo Beach, outside LA, and besides a pit stop working in a yogurt store in high school, working with animals was all she had ever known.

We met in person for the first time in Vegas. That was a no-brainer. If it didn't work out, there were plenty of things to console an addict, starting with (but certainly not limited to) gambling and all-you-can-eat buffets. I had my friend Amy at the ready with an exit strategy: when the phone rang at a prearranged time, I would find out Benny was ill, and I'd have to head back ASAP. Jill would understand that.

Of course it didn't go down that way. We laughed and laughed and this time we could collapse together into a king-size bed at the Sahara. And thank God, because it meant that when my insurance company told me that I was costing them a fortune and I had two choices, gastric bypass surgery or gastric bypass surgery, I had somebody I completely trusted to help me get through it.

Benny, meanwhile, perhaps in sympathy with me, began developing his own eating issues.

There was the time, for example, that he stopped drinking his water. Whether he was thirsty or not doesn't play into this; the fact was that I couldn't get him to drink. He already refused, under any circumstances, to eat wet food, and I can't even begin to describe this frustration, but that's another story. But because of his reliance on water instead of food for hydration, he was now constantly underhydrated, with a lot of dander, a lot of excess shedding, and his coat was really dull. And then one day, because all his regular bowls were in the dishwasher, he walked up to a small, beveled glass tumbler that I was drinking from, seemed fascinated by the way the water reflected and danced off the engraved areas . . . and drank from it. He stuck his head all the way in and started drinking like there was no tomorrow. So, no questions asked, I went out to the ninety-nine-cent store and stocked up on those glass parfait ice-cream dishes with the same kind of beveled designs on the outside that refract light, and I put them all over the place in the dual hope that he would drink more water and have another piece of territory to call his own, to make part of his daily rounds. And sure enough, he drank from them. In true Benny style, however, if I moved them *at all*, he wouldn't drink. In fact for the first several weeks I had to put little masking-tape Xs where the dishes were supposed to go—the end table, next to my bed, my nightstand, wherever—and eventually that apartment was covered in masking tape and ice-cream dishes.

Then he started pulling his fur out yet again, more vigorously than ever. The more compulsive Benny got, the less I understood him. By now this was a frustrating point of rage for me; the what, the why that sent him into fits of fur pulling, mutilating himself, was maddening. There are some behaviors that can be willfully swept under the rug. This was not one of them. This was a behavior that left scars, blood, pieces of him missing—and I could swear, when I caught him and managed to break the spell, cleaning fur trails from all around him, he looked . . . *shamed*. Like I had caught him in a destructive ritual that he had no power over.

I understood that my reading was wholly anthropomorphic and projected, and I wondered why it still resonated so deeply. And then I got it. The look I interpreted from him was no different from the look I remember giving to the pretty stranger in the supermarket parking lot, after

the kids had called me a fat fuck, as I struggled to walk
into the King Soopers to get a few frozen pizzas. And the
look she gave me back, sympathetic with a hint of "why don't
you make a different choice?" was the same look I gave
Benny, day after head-banging day. We were compulsive
mirrors; I couldn't help him, yet again, until I helped
myself. In fact, I had to walk the walk again. I always told
adopters that you are at the top of the energy food chain in
your home. Your stress becomes manifested in your animal
companions, as surely as it is manifested in your significant
other, in your children. If you choose to share your life with
others, you have a responsibility to check your shit at the
door or others will suffer. And Benny was suffering. When
was I going to learn that blind spots in him were Achilles'
heels in me?

There was a long mandatory waiting period between
scheduling the surgery and actually having it, during which
you had to go through a psych evaluation and classes. Fairly
soon before my scheduled date, I started going to Overeaters
Anonymous meetings. I gained even more weight, however,
since my lower self was making noise about going out with a
bang. The mandatory classes began ten weeks before my

date. When I say mandatory, I mean, miss one and you're done—no surgery for you.

A few days before the first class I was on the phone with Jill. "You know, I got this, kind of like, you know, my chest is tight . . ."

And she says, "You mean you have chest pains?"

"I didn't say I had chest pains, *per se*. That sounds so . . . you know . . . I just feel a little bronchial."

"How are your feet? Can you get into your shoes?"

"No."

"You need to call the doctor."

Again with the doctor thing. "Seriously, I do not want to call the doctor. I just don't want to deal with this."

But she girlfriended me into it. I called the doctor, and as soon as he heard "chest pains" and "swollen feet"—I swear I hadn't hung up the phone before I heard sirens coming down the street. And now came the humiliating nadir of my fat humiliation: I was on the third floor of a walk-up building, and they wouldn't let me walk down the stairs. They wheeled me out of my own house.

The hospital held me for three days, and on the first night the doctor did his own sleep study. The next morning, he walked in with a long tape of EKG readout.

"See this line?" he said.

"Yeah."

"That's you sleeping."

222

"Okay."

"And see this one here?"

"Yeah."

"That's your heart stopping for thirty-seven seconds."

Beat.

"I *died*?"

"Well, we prefer to see it as a rest."

"I *rested*?"

I was fucking dead. I don't care what you want to call it. I'm sure there was a white light involved.

The third day of my hospital stay was the first of the required classes, so I had my drummer pick me up and drive me screaming down to the place where it was being held, and I showed up for the first class with my hospital band still on.

It couldn't have been more movie-ready. There I am, sitting there with a hospital bracelet on, face-to-face with the rest of my class, forty people in various stages of about-to-be-deadness. And I *insisted*, gnawing that thing off my wrist, that they were SO much worse off than me, just like at that first meeting when I heard Dmitri talk of Christmas and his burned lips. But facts are facts. We were all about to be dead. If you've been in a room of people who all went into rehab around the same time, you can look around the room and say, this is what addiction really looks like. Everybody's squirming, everybody's detoxing, everybody's a drug addict.

In this room, though, I looked around and everyone had busted blood vessels in their faces, busted blood vessels in their calves and their ankles, canes, walkers, oxygen apparatus. We were all about to be dead by food. But as long as we stuck around and agreed to at least entertain the idea of learning, of breaking these chains, we might live not to see another Whopper.

My stomach surgery was done laparoscopically, which meant that I wasn't actually opened up. What they do is bypass your stomach (mine was at this point the size of a watermelon) and part of your small intestine to create a new "stomach" pouch about the size of an egg right above your hip bone. (This has had some odd side effects. For one thing, when I get full now, it's not in my belly, and that feels odd. And I don't get heartburn because I don't have stomach acid, which is great. But the downside is that food absorption doesn't happen well. You eat to get full, but you have to get most of your nutrients from other places. You have to take in about 100 grams of protein a day. You have to get your calcium from other places. You have to get your iron from other places. Which I tend to be slack about.)

So I came home and I sat in front of the TV and I was crying. This is really pathetic and awful to talk about, but I was crying and I was saying to Benny, "I want a turkey sub, I want a turkey sub," and I said it over and over and over and over again. I just wanted a turkey sub. And I thought that for the rest of my life I would never be able to eat one again. Then I made the mistake of calling Jill. She's never been one for "It's okay, honey, let's talk about it, there, there"–type shit. Her family comes from Germany by way of North Dakota. Which is to say the family motto is: "Rub some dirt in it and stop crying." Exactly what I needed at that moment in time.

Needless to say, though, the weight came pouring off me. There were some days I lost a pound, and some days I lost two. In seven months or so I lost over a hundred pounds. And I'll tell you, that really screws up your body pretty good, not to mention your self-identification. I was no longer "the big guy." I lost muscle mass, my hair went completely gray. But it was better than the alternative.

When I first got clean off drugs, there was about a two-year period during which I couldn't watch images of drug use on TV. Pot smoking, drinking, coke snorting—those were the things that triggered me, that gave me using dreams so strong I sometimes woke up with the taste of coke in the back of my throat. But my using dreams of food were so much closer to the surface, because you never recognize it as being a bad thing. Food was just something I did a little bit too much of, but it's not illegal. It's a devil you have to dance with every fucking day of your life. You have to eat food.

Now, I haven't worked my program as hard as I could have. I've gained some of that weight back. Quitting smoking didn't help. But I'm still in okay shape, and one thing that's allowed me to stay that way is seeing other people put back the entire amount of weight they lost. You can literally kill yourself doing that. But addiction is such a strong thing. I know one guy who, two weeks after the surgery, when you can only eat soft food, was putting chili cheeseburgers in a blender, blending them into a smoothie, putting it into a sippy cup, taking that to work with him, and nursing it for hours at a time. He would go out to places like Denny's with friends, and he would come with packets of Saltines, which inflate the pouch, and then you can drink soda and inflate it even more, and then you can force some food in there. And then he would excuse himself to go to the bathroom and throw up. And then he would do it again and again and again. Your addiction does not go away just because you have a pouch.

That's addiction. That's what we do.

There's a picture of me from the day before my surgery, and even though I'm smiling in the picture, there is a sense of defeat and misery in my face that I never, ever, ever want to see again. It can't be an option. I've seen pictures of me drooling, stumbling around, high, that somehow I can dismiss, and I'm not sure why that is, but I cannot do that with food. Which made me think, I may have been addicted to many things in my life, but this was the thing that I learned as a very, very young child, and this was the thing that was going to kill me. Every day of my life I know that I could go and get high again, and I know that I can go drink again, and I'll go into a tailspin and I'll have a relapse, and there's a 50–50 chance that I'll pull out of it. But I can promise you one thing: if I have a relapse that involves me gaining, say, sixty pounds, I will never come back, because I'll gain two hundred, and I'll be dead. I'll kill myself. I'm not trying to be dramatic here, but if I wind up four hundred pounds and suffering the way I was again, it will kill me or I will kill myself, because I will not do this again.

Sugar, Spice, and Everything in a Million Pieces

One of the first phone calls I got after my surgery was from this guy in Boston, a lawyer named Phil. I have no idea what brand of law Phil practiced, but it was definitely the money-making kind. He made it a point right after introducing himself to tell me how big his house was; after making me feel sufficiently like a pauper, he moved on to the problem.

The cat who'd been living with Phil for quite a while was named Sugar, so the new cat was—of course—Spice. She was a community cat from his neighborhood; he'd worked really hard on capturing her and bringing her into his home. Spice was a kitten, very loving and very adorable, and Sugar wanted to murder her.

Phil was convinced (and after hearing the recounting of

Living the Zoned Life

Permanent site swapping is a controversial idea. Shouldn't all cats have equal access to the space at all times? In a perfect world, yes.

In this world, certain cats just don't like certain other cats, and we can't make them get along. If you want to keep both of them, live a tightly regimented zoned existence. If one of them sleeps with you one night, the other one gets the next night.

In the cat world, separate but equal is okay. Your only other option is to consider re-homing one of the cats.

The key here is not what's best for *you* but what's best for *them*.

the violence, I agreed) that there was no way I could do the job from Boulder, so he said, "I'll fly you in first class, put you up in a suite, and pay you $1,200 plus expenses. You spend the weekend with me and my wife and two cats and just, please, make it work." I had never had anybody offer me that much money before—the most I'd ever had in my pocket in my life was $200—and the idea of making $1,200 for a weekend's worth of doing what I liked rather than for

moving rocks from one end of the lot to another in a wheelbarrow seemed to be a message from the universe that I was
on the right track.

So I went to Boston and, after picking me up at Logan and
taking me out to dinner, Phil explained, with a dry, acerbic
wit, what was going on. Underneath the W. C. Fields–like
put-on about hating kids and barely tolerating anybody or
anything else, he was very serious about this issue, and the
strain on his marriage was approaching the breaking point.
His wife didn't see why they couldn't just find a home for this
nice kitten, but he was *convinced* it was going to work—why
wouldn't it work?—and then he started in with the whole
you're-our-only-hope-if-you-can't-do-this-I-have-no-
idea-what-we're-going-to-do-because-I-love-this-kid-
so-much thing. We were walking back to his late-model Benz
import, white, sleek, admittedly beautiful, when I looked
down and saw, no joke, a pair of brass balls hanging from the
rear bumper, the kind usually reserved for the trailer hitch
of an F-350 like you see on the back roads of Iowa.

When we got to his house, before I had the chance to say I
wanted to spend some time alone with the cats, which
would've been the smart thing to do, I let him and his wife
tag along and show me the place, which deserved its own zip
code. The hugeness was magnified because it wasn't clut-
tered with stuff, just clean lines and shades of white all
around. A beautiful house right on a golf course—one of

those enclaves where you imagine an entire neighborhood landing in the middle of nowhere, just like a UFO.

Ten minutes into meeting the cats I realized that I had my work cut out for me, but I didn't think anything I tried was going to do any good. The resident cat, Sugar, wanted the other one dead. I'm usually the king of the silver lining who says, I know if Sugar wanted Spice dead that she'd be dead by now. Well, if Phil hadn't kept them separated, living a zoned existence, methodically switching them out in regular intervals—she'd have been dead by now. But Phil was hell-bent on creating the picture he saw in his head of everybody being a happy family.

So twenty-four hours into my visit I'm trying every technique that I know to reintroduce cats, but I feel like I'm going through the motions. Because now that I've lost my protective bulk, the world is closer . . . and I don't know what to do with it. This is the curse of lifting the veil: you can't exist as a cookie-cutter advice-giver anymore. I know plenty of behaviorists, veterinarians, doctors, teachers, people who have lost their inspiration, who do it by the numbers. Their work is done remotely through phone or e-mail or both. They say okay, well, you have problem a, b, or c, this is how you deal with it, and they recite the same thing that they've been reciting for twenty years. But I couldn't do that. The veil can only be lifted, not dropped. You can't go back. And when the veil comes up, it's not just about knowing cats better—you're more open to emotional states of any kind. And the human psychology involved here was talking as loudly as the cat psychology.

That night I called Karl from my hotel room. "I'm trying so hard," I said.

"You shouldn't be trying. You should know by now that your efforts to control the world are irrelevant to those living in that world."

"No, I mean, honestly, I'm doing everything I know how to do, but these cats don't want to be together."

"Jackson, it's not the cats who don't want to be together. The universe doesn't want you to put this together. It's not meant to be put together. These cats don't like each other. They're trying to send everybody a message, and nobody's listening."

I didn't want to accept this. I pictured Phil, his wife, the cats, all doing some happily-ever-after dance, and I decided, just like Phil, that I would make that picture happen, no matter what. I began a food reintroduction plan, and they were doing pretty well. In fact, these cats were two feet away from each other, on opposite sides of the door, and they were doing just fine. But when you opened the door or when they ran out of food, Sugar went to murder Spice. She would chase her through the massive house and I would tear ass after them up the stairs, down the stairs, into the garage, and you would lose track of where they were until you heard the screaming.

Cat Reintroduction 101

When two cats have fallen out, the way to reintroduce them is by using positive association—which means food!

Feed the two cats on either side of a door so they understand they only smell each other when they get food, and they only get food when they smell each other. "Hmm," they'll start thinking, "maybe this other cat isn't so bad."

Gradually move the bowls closer, keeping each on the opposite side of the door. Then crack the door to add a visual element to the reintroduction. You're on your way!

The next day I'm in one of the huge bathrooms with Sugar. And while Spice is running around—she's a kitten, she's not buying into this drama, she just doesn't care—Sugar's locked up in the bathroom tossing off the stink eye to me from the top of a cat tree in the corner. I start talking to her, saying in increasingly desperate tones, "Pretty please, I am out of ideas here. Your dad spent $1,200 to get me here and he doesn't quite know yet that I'm a fraud. You have got to help me out. Please get along with this kitten. Dammit."

And I let her out the door of the bathroom and I felt like she was with me, but the second she saw that kitten, all bets were off and I was chasing after her up the stairs down the stairs until Spice was cornered up on the dining room table.

The awful thing was that the worse these sessions went, the more absolutely *verklempt* Phil became; finally, his stress level was interfering with the process so badly that I banished him from the house. His wife and I could do the sessions while he walked around the block. And the cats got better when it was just me and Jessica. They didn't become best friends, but you could feel the storm cloud lift. And then Phil would come back in with his nervousness, his doom and gloom, and the fact that he was a walking ultimatum ruined everything.

To put it mildly, it was a complete failure.

So at the end of the day I gave them tools, I gave them options, but I told them I didn't see these cats ever wanting to live together. I couldn't *make* this happen, nobody could make this happen. I don't think I could have reached this understanding before getting totally clean—the understanding that this was not about me being a success or failure or fraud or genius, but only about these two cats and what they needed. In previous consults, when I knew things were falling apart, I would just cut bait. I would just do the basics of the consult and never check back in because I knew it was going to fail and I didn't want to examine why. But now I *couldn't* not examine why, because it was staring me in the face.

I suggested a zoned existence for the cats.

"Absolutely not," said Phil. "There's no way. I'm never going to do that."

"Ok," I said dubiously, "you can keep working this program, but . . ." I didn't have the guts to tell him he was using the cats as fodder for his pride, the same way we use a child or a dog or a house or anything else that can't talk back. And it's fine with a house; you can validate your success by building a huge house on the banks of a golf course, but you cannot force sentient beings into the shape you want them to take.

Phil called me about six months later and said that Jessica had left him. He said it was all about the cats, that he saw a life with both Sugar and Spice, and Jessica just didn't get it, so she left him. And not only did she leave him, but she took up with another guy who lived on the tenth hole, and he would see them from his solarium, he said, "drinking mimosas on Sunday mornings on the deck of this new guy's house."

But we all know that they didn't get divorced over the cats. I think he felt her slipping away from him and he made a doubled-up effort to create a fortress, a manifestation of a happy home, and those two cats were part of that manifestation, along with home improvements and perfectly cooked dinners with candlelight. He had a picture in his head of what life should look like and she, goddammit, was going to follow him, and these two cats, goddammit, were going to follow him.

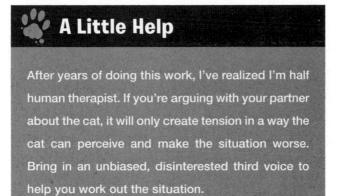

A Little Help

After years of doing this work, I've realized I'm half human therapist. If you're arguing with your partner about the cat, it will only create tension in a way the cat can perceive and make the situation worse. Bring in an unbiased, disinterested third voice to help you work out the situation.

I think Phil's a fantastic guy. I love him. I still hear from him. But I'm also sad, because he still expects, nine or ten years later, that someday these two cats are going to get together. They've spent a decade site swapping—which, by the way, I see no problem with—but the thing I find so distressing is that they've had to live their whole lives feeling the energy of the disappointment of human expectation.

New and
Still Breaking

Benny had come to me with a shattered pelvis, and like any other traumatic physical alteration, it changed his physiology. As I've mentioned, declaw a cat and it'll change his physiology forever. Think about it: if you cut off one of your toes, you'd walk differently for the rest of your life. You can't rehab a cat's broken pelvis; you just live with it. Staying in a cage for a few weeks doesn't put everything back to normal. So by the time Benny was seven or eight, he was pretty gimpy with arthritis. Remember, in the wild, cats' job in life is to hide pain—they're literally dead meat if they display any vulnerability—so though he tried not to show it, as time went on, year by year, one of his paws began to atrophy and become misshapen from the compensation, and he started to have some trouble. He groomed the malformed leg even more obsessively than he always had, and when he was in

pain he would often stop in the middle of a stride and collapse, his mouth around the offending appendage.

There were also geographical problems, because in Colorado we don't just have winter, we have Winter, and we don't
just have altitude, we have Altitude. The resulting barometric swings wreaked havoc on Benny's joints and broken
places, leaving him even more attached to the earth than
normal—an *über*-bush dweller. He would have nothing at all
to do with jumping, not even on the couch or bed, so I made
sure his bush beds were plentiful, and heated. The litter
box, too, would sometimes become unfriendly, but I had an
idea about that, too. When Rabbi was dying of diabetes, he
had developed a peripheral neuropathy, so he walked on his
hocks (the cat equivalent of knees), and it made getting in
and out of the litter box ridiculous. It was then that I discovered the puppy litter box—spacious, with a dipped opening
in the front that was just a few inches above floor level. It
was perfect for Rabbi, and now it proved equally perfect for
Benny during the challenging times.

Once again, I kept trying to find one hallelujah cause,
kept trying to tie everything together. These aren't things
that exist in a vacuum, I decided, these are symptoms of one
root problem. (I often did this in my consults, too. I didn't
consider, for instance, that a cat could be peeing outside the
box in the same location for two different reasons—because

she's threatened by outside intruders, for example, and because the intruders have upped her stress levels to the point where she's developed a urinary tract infection. Which is not very sound science at all, but I'm not a sound scientist.) So if Benny was pulling out fur and it was wintertime I would check his arthritis; if he was missing the litter box I would manipulate his joints trying to find pain where often pain didn't exist.

For about seven months I theorized. This is what I tend to do. I jotted notes, I said, "Come on, Benny, talk to me," staring at him, resorting to telepathy. . . . But as I gathered the symptoms and made a whiteboard out of his symptomatology—don't ask me why I hadn't learned my lesson by now, hadn't figured out a way to ignore that well-known behaviorist's voice telling me I needed to do this scientifically or not at all—it just didn't add up.

And eventually I said, screw it, I'm just going to deal with the symptoms. So I began to look at things in terms of cues. If he's giving me this cue then I have to look in this direction. I couldn't always be looking for a touchdown pass, a discovery that, oh, my God, all of these six symptoms together mean that he's foreseeing his own death through hanging. Because whenever I thought I'd found one, he'd be like, *you idiot*, and he would do something that proved it couldn't be that.

In the end, the key for me, once again, was empathy—working from the neck down instead of from the neck up. So going back to an instinctual and empathetic place, I said, how would I want to be touched if I were in pain? So I thought, he's been living with a broken pelvis for all those years during Colorado winters. I've got bad knees, I know what that feels like, so I started giving him what I thought I would want, which was heat and traction. I would rub my hands together to create friction heat, and then I would wrap my hands around his whole underside, and I cradled his pelvis. But uniform pressure on cats tends to freak them out, so I also pulled a little bit, stayed active instead of static, because the fact is, they've got to trust that touch. And finally, with the addition of a Spirit Essences formula called Creak-Away and occasionally some anti-inflammatory medicine, I was able to keep his arthritis at bay as much as I could.

The good thing was that this process did lead me to some cool discoveries. I wouldn't have found animal chiropractic work, for example, if it hadn't been for Benny's pelvis. I was looking for any help with the problem. I had a history with bodywork so I could practice qigong, craniosacral massage, energy release, but these are subtle modalities, and he didn't like them. He rebelled against subtlety at all times in his life. Energetic information has to be collected and processed. He had no time for that. Chiropractic,

Stroking Versus Holding

If you stroke cats, there's an end in sight, and they like that. If there's no end in sight—it's not a stroke but a hold—that tends to tense them up more than relax them. (It's totally the opposite with dogs. With dogs you can hold them and they'll melt into your hold. And that's the theory behind products like the Anxiety Wrap or the Thundershirt—feeling swaddled calms dogs.) In another example of being a cat detective, just like finding the sweet spot in your vocal range that works for your cat, do the same with your touch—what degree of pressure relaxes her and which touch, like the big hug, makes her shrink back, twitch, or head for the hills?

though—you're being manipulated, and there's nothing subtle about it.

But it took me months. I kept theorizing and overthinking and making charts, because I had that animal behaviorist's voice in my head, I had my father's voice in my head, I felt I had something to prove, when what I actually had was a cat who needed me not to think but to feel.

. . .

As Benny got older, he began to get sick more and more often. The first time I ever saw his asthma in action is impossible to forget. I had that moment when he was hacking and I was hovering over him going, vet or no vet? Vet or no vet? Vet or no vet? And then I instinctively took two fingers and rubbed his throat up and down; I just wanted him to pass whatever it was. And my rubbing actually did relax his throat a little bit, and the hacking stopped, but it was only coincidence, and the hacking kept coming back. Thank God for the Internet, because when I started googling I found Fritz the Brave. Fritz and his guardian are now gone, but fritzthebrave.com is still an invaluable resource. On the Web site there was a video of Fritz having an asthma attack and it was identical to what was happening to Benny. It looked like he was trying to put up a hair ball but there was no wetness to it whatsoever, it was just a hacking dryness, nothing was ever brought up.

So I started doing research on asthma, and I called Jean, and I started doing things like changing from clay litter. This had an immediate effect, because there wasn't this plume of ash and dust every time I'd pour the litter out of the bag or every time he'd scratch in it. I also took the hoods off the litter boxes so that at least the dust still there would disperse through the apartment instead of getting stuck around the box itself.

Don't Be a Litterbug!

Clay litter isn't just bad for cats' health. In addition to the problems it can cause for cats with asthma, it also contains silica, which causes cancer in cats and humans. Furthermore, the clay it's made from is usually mined in a way that damages the environment, and once you throw clay litter away it never biodegrades in the landfill—it will be here long after we humans are dead and gone.

I tried to change from dry to wet food, to raise the water content in his body, but naturally, he being the cat he was, no matter what wet food I put down—and I tried every last brand—he would walk up, sniff it, and gag. Wet food and Sharpies: he consistently gagged. Finally—*finally*—I discovered that he would eat Whole Foods deli-case herb-roasted turkey. And that was *it*. No turkey from the regular supermarket, no Whole Foods smoked turkey. It was Whole Foods deli-case herb-roasted turkey or nothing.

This was infuriating, because dry food irritated his lungs and his trachea. I was able to go to a grain-free food, but it was still inherently dry. So we tried to hydrate him with a portable nebulizer, twice, and each time he panicked so badly at the sight of that mask that he had an asthma attack twice as bad as it had ever been. His typical attacks could last a few minutes—two, three, four minutes—but both times we tried to use the asthma medication with that big mask, an attack would last ten to twelve minutes, until he was really gasping for air, and it just wasn't worth it. So for the rest of his life he was on our Easy-Breather from Spirit Essences, and usually prednisone. But the asthma never went away.

Once my weight came off, and *I* was breathing for the first time in years, I opened to the idea that Benny's, Velouria's, and my time in Boulder might be at an end. The music scene had been shifting for years away from bands toward dance music, and besides, sober I just didn't have the manic energy—or the need—to get up onstage wearing a diaper and a baseball cap with a blinking bicycle light on it and recite a thirteen-minute monologue underscored by hypnotic music from my band. Hell, let's face it: the only thing keeping me in Boulder was my inability to own my life enough to pack my shit and go.

Cat Daddy

My first trip to visit Jill (rather than to hook up in some mutually convenient city) was to help guide her when her dog Reilly was going terribly downhill and she couldn't face the decision to let him go. I felt her pain and his, and was on a plane the next night. It was the Fourth of July. As I descended into the LA area at exactly 9:00 p.m., fireworks exploded with socioeconomic impunity, fire in the sky from Compton to Manhattan Beach. Of course I believe in signs; this was going to be my next stop. After all, I had been making a long, slow crawl across the country for more than twenty years. Why not go from sea to shining sea?

I knew Reilly for less than twenty-four hours. He was a fairly enormous yellow Lab. Reilly was the alpha of Jill's pretty-damned-populated home (when I showed up, there were five dogs and eight cats), but he was immobilized. It was so sad. She loved him so strongly and he was patently unable to perform his "job." He couldn't direct traffic. He couldn't walk. I carried him to the car. I carried him into the vet while Jill waited, hysterically crying, in the car. I was his guardian in those last minutes. As I would find out quickly, Jill's work life was just like mine—there was no down time. She still had to work that day, completely shrouded in grief. When she finished, we held hands, and in the dark, punctuated by a few fires, we made our way to the waves of the Pacific on Hermosa Beach. I waded in up to my calves.

And in that moment, my notoriously noisy mind, the city

that I had been seeking escape from for fifteen years in the mountains of Colorado, went deafeningly silent.

It was a completely ecstatic feeling. After all this time, I remembered that I came from an island. I was a water person, living in exile among ice-climbing earth worshippers.

I was ready to go.

The physical part of the move to California was a piece of cake for me. I was, after all, *ready*. I had spent fifteen years in the place voted by my inner city best place to have a complete nervous breakdown. I had had said breakdown, wallowed in it for years, and then embarked on a radical and redefining journey of regaining my marbles while shedding my addictions. It was time, and I was *so* not scared; I could taste the glory of change, the promise of life at the other shining sea.

Of course, just because I was ready to go doesn't mean I was ready to go. I fought like hell to keep change at bay. The only way I'd move to California, I told Jill, was if she could find a place in her area no more than three blocks from the beach. We had to have a yard for her dogs. We couldn't spend any more than two thousand dollars a month together. I put enough obstacles in the way to make the goal unattainable. But Jill rose to the challenge and found us a home.

Cat Daddy

Once I accepted the inevitable, the only thing that had me stressed in the least was Benny. As we've established, he wasn't exactly the king of smooth adaptation from place to place; move his dinner bowl and he might turn into Gandhi. I felt like I had to cover every conceivable base, so that he would make it to the promised land in one piece.

I call it the promised land not so lightly, either; Benny was not well. By now, his asthma was often completely debilitating. He had also begun to "snarfle"—there was a problem in his sinuses now as well as in his bronchial tubes. The most heartbreaking aspect of this came when he would cuddle up to me, in itself a phenomenon that had only manifested in recent years, and begin to purr. Inevitably the love would get too big; the purr would take over, and one end or another of the broken breather would rebel and cause an awful gag and choke. His eyes bulging, he would swallow hard and regain his cat composure. It had taken Benny so many years to settle into his *felinity*—I felt horrible that now it was almost like he was being punished for embracing it. The promised land meant the move from the climatic unbearable, at least from Benny's perspective. No more bone-crunching winters, no more dry apartment heat, no more airless altitude. Benny's life would be spent breathing in sea-level humidity, sipping in oxygen like it was a giant fruity cocktail served up in a tiki-head glass.

Now, we just had to get him there.

Cat Travel 101

When you travel with your cat, make sure you embark prepared!

1. Put together a go kit with food, no-spill bowls, harnesses, disposable litter boxes, bottled water, and a feline first-aid kit (in mine I have gauze, instant ice pack, mini-scissors, quickstop, thermal blanket, hydrogen peroxide, tweezers, Q-tips, eye wash, eye dropper, emery board, and antibiotics).
2. Travel with copies of your cat's medical records. Don't wait for the last minute to request them from your vet!
3. Research pet-friendly lodging before you make any reservations.
4. Make sure he's microchipped and tagged with your current address information (your new address, if the travel is a move).
5. As you plan your route, check out shelters on the Web, just in case you get separated!
6. Pack photos of your cat in case you need to show people what he looks like.

Cat Daddy

I decided that I would rent a U-Haul trailer and hitch it to my Blazer, and whatever would fit, would fit. That would leave the Blazer itself for Jill and me, and I would flatten the seats in the back to make a home away from home for Velouria and Benny. Dishes, litter boxes, familiar scents. It was so important to keep a sense of sameness throughout what would undoubtably be a tough couple of weeks.

That trailer was packed so tightly, in true gypsy style, that I actually had to toss my couch. My one symbol of grown-upness, my king-size bed, also had to be put aside. My plants had made it, at least, but that trailer had not one single cubic foot left in it. I might be a gypsy, but I'm also a guy; I know how to pack the hell out of a car.

I timed the trip so that I had to stop for gas ten miles out—once again Benny's doing. I had learned that, no matter what I ever tried, within the first seven miles of any trip, Benny would poop, puke, or both. So you just went with that particular flow. You waited for the inevitable, stopped, cleaned it up, and you were on your way. By the time I gassed up, I also was wiping the back of the Blazer clean. Then, it was onward and upward.

But it was 100 degrees that Labor Day weekend, and I was driving that 2000 Blazer up I-70 on a steep, long hill out of Boulder Valley, dragging that trailer chock-full of my life. You do the math. It was precisely at the worn sign that proclaimed "Buffalo Bill's Burial Site Ahead" that the smoke

Ward off Carsickness!

If your animal gets carsick, it's pet detective time again. Here are some things you can experiment with:

1. Make sure she associates the carrier with good things—take her fun places in it, try feeding her in it—before you leave for your destination!
2. Try a smaller or a larger carrier.
3. Give her more or less visual access.

began pouring from under the hood. Then the unmistakable sugary smell of antifreeze. And then, the gas pedal just stopped gassing. The choice was to pull over or risk gravity taking the four of us back to the valley floor.

"Can you get out here?" I said to AAA on the phone. "I need to get this car to a mechanic."

"A mechanic? On Labor Day? You're kidding, right?"

Shit.

"Just send a tow for a Blazer and a packed trailer. We'll take it from there."

And then, as Jill put Benny and Velouria in their carriers

and got them out of the overheating car, a swarm of bees descended on us.

I had to walk away. I was trying to demonstrate my adaptive abilities to the woman I was moving decidedly far away from my comfort zone to live with, and *this* was what was happening? How was she going to have faith in me to handle things? (Never mind that my ability to handle things not having to do with cats or guitars was pretty much purely theoretical at this point.)

I'm not sure what exactly I began to mutter. In the prism of my recollection, it was the Serenity Prayer, but in reality it could well have been the Gettysburg Address.

"Oh, God," Jill later told me she said to her mother on the cell phone. "Jackson's talking to a telephone pole. Whoops, no. Jackson's *yelling* at a telephone pole." Once again, I make the courageous choice to change my life, and once again the god of cars throws a two-ton monkey wrench at my good intentions. Or maybe the universe was telling me, not so gently, that it was time to surrender.

As the tow truck pulled us into the Boulder U-Haul, Benny began to pant. As I picked up the phone to call Jean and ask her what to do since Benny was about to die and I couldn't do anything right, I remembered that even though it was 100 degrees outside I had put an old cable-knit sweater he loved in his carrier. I turned to tell Jill to get it out of there, but she was already doing it, because he had crapped in there again. I guess it had been seven miles from Buffalo Bill's grave site. At least he was still performing like a Swiss watch. That was reassuring. Gag-inducing, but reassuring.

All we could get from U-Haul was a small panel truck, which meant we went from the entire rear of the Blazer for the cats to literally nothing. No backseat, nothing. Their carriers were piled on top of each other in between our seats. And it took forever to get this rental, so not only was my perfectly planned cat trip going to absolute shit, but we had to spend the night at a crappy roadside motel in Arizona. I mean, we couldn't exactly be choosy; the cats were deal-breakers at many a fine establishment.

I concealed my fear of Benny's adjustment to this new place underneath a tidy internal to-do list. Get cats in, get cat-and-Jackson-scented blankets on the bed. Get scratching post out from back of truck, position it by door for territorial security. Get litter box in, set dishes up on counter with food and canisters like they've always lived there, execute dinner ritual like every single night.

Benny wouldn't eat.

I could barely disguise my outright panic. The only thing that stopped me from heading outside to talk to a telephone pole was my knowledge of his needs. I had to center myself. I concentrated on feeding Velouria, hoping that he would follow her lead. He wouldn't. And I would not let him sway my center. Acting as if it were a regular night, we settled in, watching TV in the desert dark. And, as the day began to fade into sleep, I heard the crunching of dry cat food and a slight snarfle. Phew.

Once we were in our new place, Jill and I had mixed success in brady bunching our pets. Kalee, Jill's older black Lab, *always* deferred—six-pound Velouria whacked her in the snout once and from that day forward she simply turned her head away whenever one of the cats made eye contact. Jill's cats Chips and Tom quickly developed working relationships with Benny and Velouria.

But Zeke, Jill's third cat, only two weeks on the scene, was twenty pounds of bully. He'd been bullying Chips since setting foot in the place and when Benny arrived he was just more low-hanging fruit. Karma from Benny's domination of Rabbi and Velouria years before had come back to bite him in the ass. So in a true test of the methods I'd been working for years, we zoned the 950-square-foot beach house and site swapped religiously. But nothing in my new home was cut-and-dried. Sure, I could keep Zeke away from Benny and Velouria, which was wise; Velouria was back to pulling her "run like prey" routine in this unfamiliar spot, and every time Benny came face-to-face with his nemesis/challenger, his snarfling betrayed his alpha facade. He'd bow his chest out in challenge to the punk in the alley, and the bowing would make him cough. Old man, you ain't what you used to be. And Zeke would charge. It was, of course, both familiar and necessary to establish long-term stability.

But I was human, not just a detached robot observer. It made me so totally unhappy to see my poor boy stressed and defeated in an alien space. Furthermore, although Benny had eaten at the hotel, he decided that would be the last time, at least for that particular brand. "This particular taste in my mouth," he might as well have been saying, "reminds me of the time you shoved me in a carrier with not enough space and made me crap on a wool sweater in 100-degree heat, so no thanks, I'll pass."

So the fevered experimentation began. Cats on hunger strike can be awfully scary: too fat and they are prone to hepatic lipidosis, or fatty liver disease, which is often fatal. Too skinny, like Benny, and you can see the negative wasting effects after just two missed meals. Thank god for the California phenomenon El Pollo Loco; he loved and devoured their chicken, so though I had to mix it with dry food (shockingly, fast-food chicken isn't nutritionally complete for cats), at least I got him eating again.

Unfortunately, as much as I really felt amazing in my new life at the water's edge, where I most definitely belonged,

Benny was going downhill. Even though I had provided a better climate, his body was just not happy—the straw was crimping at both ends: his mouth/nose and his lungs. I continued to look for ways to circumvent the anatomical realities—I took him to new vets, both holistic and traditional. Acupuncture seemed to provide some relief for his stressed-out breathing, but, having just relocated my practice to a brand-new area, I wasn't making enough money, and I couldn't afford treatments every few weeks. He began to have trouble smelling his food well enough to be interested in it. I took to putting El Pollo Loco chicken in a food processor and making a paste, which I would then heat up just a bit to release the scent, and then I would put it on top of his dry food. Eventually this was filed, as so much would be, under "good intentions."

In retrospect I guess I didn't even see him slipping and sliding. I was used to his various manifestations, the pulling, the whining, the grouchy outbursts; I just wasn't used to looking for the subtle signs of surrender. It was literally weeks before I realized he was doing the absolute minimum—food to litter to brown bed. Lather, rinse, repeat. Benny actually stopped overgrooming himself. Not because he was "cured"—that would just be too perfect and naive. He had begun to surrender. And it maddened me. Because even though I circled surrender in a mating dance as if it were the summer sex and perfume smell of my first love, I had no idea what to do when it said yes. Of course I made it about me. We only hate things, traits, defects, *the beings* that remind us of our own struggles, the things we hate about our deepest selves.

Jill indulged my manic quest—oh, yes, I never stopped— for the answer, the "something" that would make him better. I experimented like mad to find a litter that was dust-free, made of natural ingredients, and unscented, yet clumped and retained scent well enough for use by five cats, one of which had renal failure and peed like a racehorse. (Hint: said litter doesn't exist.) I ran humidifiers in every room. I was chopping, supplementing, turning his food into warm stew that could get through the crimped straw of his sinuses. The boy had taken the path of least resistance, and I was spewing every ounce of resistance I could summon onto that path.

One night, when Jill and I got back from a dinner out, I bent over Benny to kiss his head and saw that his right pupil was completely dilated.

Don't. Panic. He'll feel it.

I wouldn't give in to the weakness in my legs. I would not, goddammit, fall. Here lies one of the lessons that have assimilated into my thick head only as I write this: I would not feel the truth in that moment, the truth being that there was undoubtedly a tumor somewhere in his sinus passage, pushing against the optic nerves. The unifying theory that I had searched for was right there, but it wasn't what I wanted to see. This was my addict, coming back to gloat. This was the result of my best thinking for years and years. My best thinking got me into strange beds, strange bars, ingesting strange things, waking up in vomit or in a hospital bed. Now, because I couldn't bear the truth, and now, when the universe manifested the defining clue so insanely fast after all of this buildup, I resorted to a classic New York City survival technique: turn your eyes down and cross to the other side of the street.

"I got it," I told Jill, already feeling her eyes roll behind me. "I know something has to be wrong with his tooth." I had seen a forensic dentist talking about some murder mystery on some murder mystery reality show and the next thing you know—it's gotta be his tooth. "He has a rotten tooth that's abscessing, and the abscess is basically leaking this poison into his nasal cavity and causing his eye to react." But I wanted, *needed* confirmation. It was 8:00 on Sunday night. Confirmation was not forthcoming.

The next morning, the veterinary dental specialist seemed to understand me. He knew instinctively that I had been to eight different vets in eight months, looking for answers that were acceptable to me. He smiled wanly after a cursory exam. "There's nothing wrong with his teeth, but there's definitely something wrong with his eye. Maybe we need to get him across the hall to the eye doctor?"

This kind of hospital was a wet dream for a conspiracy theorist like I was becoming. "Sure, let's do it."

"Jackson," said the eye doctor, "there is something for sure happening here, but without being able to anesthetize him, I can't get the images we need. And with his breathing issues, I can't guarantee that he'll come out of the anesthesia." I was nodding the whole time. Then came the worst part, the part that I was not in any way ready to hear: "I think you just need to make sure he's kept comfortable."

. . . And It's All About Me

He's not dead yet, but clearly not here. The concept of "keeping him comfortable" really is just about the waiting. And the watching. And the constant stab and restab of the diagnostic scalpel in the hands of a guy who's not a doctor but plays one on TV.

In these moments when my brain relaxes long enough to let the anger and sadness take hold, I realize that I haven't cried for Benny. I've willed him to health so many times over his life that I just assumed I'd do it again. But now my will itself is presenting as a disease, corroding my contact points with the earth on one end and the universe on the other. And my gray-and-white gift/curse/friend/teacher (oh, and cat) suffers for it.

I have felt, at my worst moments in the past few months, that the universe was mocking me. Every time I felt a secret was being leaked from the sky or earth directly to me, I've gone running to my medical friends or hustled Benny into someone else's office so that they could tell me they didn't know and couldn't find out.

"So in essence," I've found myself saying over and over, "I just stressed him out to no end to bring him here, paid you the money I needed for rent, and you're saying that all you can do is hold a piece of tissue in front of his face, say 'hmmm—see, breathing compromised a bit,' and send me on my way?"

We have to towel him twice a day, to give him antibiotics, bronchial dilators, steroids, appetite stimulants, painkillers, and fucking children's nose drops. And what hurts most of all from this is that I'm buying into this fucking mockery. I'm trying to pill the hurt away instead of actually listening. Because the "cat listener," or whisperer, or shrink—it's all a pile of steaming bullshit in the face of losing my little man. All of my learning, all of the intuition I've been so blessed in having and honing—all gone. After being clean and sober these seven-and-a-half years, in this moment all of the tools I've learned and applied in recovery just aren't as good right now as being high, or at the very least, numb. I want to numb my pain and Benny's into submission.

I do what I do so well when the storm hits: I go into the cellar and lock it down tight so I can get through my days, work, and not lose my mind. That's how I do the storm.

But Karl keeps calling, pulling that Jewish grandmother shtick that works like a charm every time. And thank God it does. When I speak to him I realize I'm in the storm cellar. I honestly haven't known it until now. I spin around and realize there are no windows, no daylight. No spiritual life, just powdered eggs and bare lightbulbs. And most important, I've left Benny in the storm while I stayed below and "strategized."

Coming up from the storm cellar has its drawbacks. Every conversation with someone close to me inevitably involves a moment of choke-and-swallow that I have to self-consciously get past, like some sort of emotional Tourette's syndrome. One of the things that must have drawn me to cats in the first place was recognizing them in me. We are predators and prey, and as such, emotional stealth, depth, and timing are crucial to our survival. Allowing the anguish of what I feel to surface scares me as much as losing Benny. I fear the raw-skin scraping of loss like a feral cat in an open field fears a coyote he knows is waiting to pounce.

When the feral and the coyote decide to surface and begin their dance from the depths of the storm cellar, those moments of choke-and-swallow come closer and closer, like contractions. Then, inevitably, driving down Sepulveda from Brentwood to the beach, the walnut shell cracks audibly and all of the things I fear consume and taunt me in front of weekend commuters. I keep thinking that I should pull over so I don't kill myself or someone else. But while the shell around my spirit may have cracked, being in the car with the windows rolled up allows insulation. The rain outside provides camouflage for the rain inside. I wail and punch the dashboard in peace.

Not to make a joyful comparison, but there's a time, after particularly good afternoon sex and the kind of joint orgasm that you only read about in *Penthouse* Forum as a kid, where you roll on your back and look out the window . . . the greens are greener, the sky is beyond vibrant. The world is in high-def, your glasses are clean. Again, not joyful, but the breath I draw is blessedly potent and the exhale clean like a beginning.

I'm grateful for the moment because I am able to say to myself, "It's not about you, genius. This is not about the meta, reforming the health-care system, formulating theories, and proving yourself right (or, conversely, wallowing in the misery of being proven wrong). This is about Benny in his dying days and just as you appreciated him at his most vibrant, appreciate him now."

My friend, a house-call vet, is about to go away for a long weekend. I don't know that Benny will make it till he gets back. There are more days than not when Benny doesn't leave his "safe bed," a brown fleece donut on the foot of our chaise where he has a good vantage point, surveying the comings and goings of all of the other animals and humans from a slight remove. In the few weeks since his condition began to worsen, the laundry list has seemed to compound daily. His eating is iffy even with the help of appetite stimulants. On bad days he doesn't groom, so his coat is losing all luster, dry with flecks of dander. His condition has compromised his breathing so he's constantly congested. When I hold and comfort him, he purrs, which sets off the snarfle reaction.

Amazingly, my friends Doug and Lindsay are going through the same thing with their beloved cat Barbra. Doug calls to see if I'll drive over to their place just to observe Babs and help them gain perspective. "We don't want Babs to suffer for three days," he says, "just so she can die with a measure of peace at home on Monday."

I tell Doug I can't do it—I'm neck-deep in Benny. "But listen, you know Barbra. You've lived with her for fifteen years. You know when the time is right. It's about her, not about you. If you make this about you, I can promise you that she will suffer more than your ego. Most important, live up to the bargain you made; you gave her a good life. Give her a good death, and don't let the release happen on her worst day. Don't let that happen." Over the years, I explain, I've seen so many guardians bring their pets into the shelter for a private euthanasia, and they've simply waited too long, a product of their own denial. The thing that's always struck me is that the person has been a portrait of emotional confusion and pain, living with the knowledge that they would have to decide When It's Time. That confusion is constantly reflected back to them as physical pain to match their emotions.

And then I realize, as I hang up with Doug, that I'm talking to myself, too.

That night, we're toweling the boy to give him meds, and I'm feeling nothing but angry. Angry is such an easy place to go. No matter how hard I've run from it my entire life, it's in my DNA. Looking down at him struggling, with all of the meds carefully lined up in a row, it's my turn to hold and Jill's to administer. We surely don't want him associating one of us with this twice-daily torture. I'm angry at the doctors—if they could only see the suffering they prescribed in such an offhanded way, if they could only see how they abuse the trust of their patients, both human and animal. And then Jill puts those nose drops in his nose—maybe one drop too many—and he jerks violently, gasping because we've momentarily cut off his precious breath. And I glare. An entire lifetime of being afraid of my own potential for violence, my ability to scream horrible things at others has made me very good at glaring. Silently, with that glare, I condemn Jill with precise and overwhelming ferocity. Jill doesn't glare, she gets pissed like normal people do, and tells me in no uncertain terms what to do with my glare.

I'm ready to boil over when I have a sudden and almost

comical moment of recognition. I'm aping the exact con-
demnation I've always flung like so much monkey shit at the
human medical industry: "Keep us sick, medicate us, keep
your pockets lined; it's your fault that I'm hooked on pills!"
I'm back to being a rabid, steering wheel–grabbing addict.
This isn't anyone's fault; this is the universe telling me to
hit my knees. This is me resisting surrender. I look down at
the helplessly swaddled being, emptied by human fear and
his own body of everything that made him my best cat frenemy so long ago. "Done," I say to Jill, carrying him back to
the bedroom. "This fucking charade," I hiss, not raising my
voice in a vain attempt not to poison the air, "this godfor-
saken farce." I walk in the opposite direction. Just to be
away. I want to smash the table and the bottles on it, but for
once I have to go directly in the opposite direction of my
own best thinking. She knows that even my surrender usually looks angry.

This is over. It's time to keep Benny *comfortable*. That
means no more appetite stimulants. No steroids. No more
torture disguised as wellness. Benny is dying and my job is
to let him. The universe has our time together on a short
leash. Let's make that time free of artifice, I think.

And now that my ego is released from its cage so it can
go crap in someone else's living room, my true self is free
to be with my boy in his final days. I tell him at our first moment of solitude that he doesn't have to tough it out any-

more, and I won't either. In a move that surprises the shit out of me, in a time when everything seems to be surprising the shit out of me, I ask him for a favor: "Please, bud, just *tell me*." I look around to make sure we're alone. I don't even want Jill to hear. "When it's time, I promise. We'll make it better before it hurts. You won't ever hurt. You just have to give me something. It'll be our special code. I promise I'll listen hard. You won't have to say it twice. Deal?"

Once given that talk, it didn't take him long.

It's 4:12 a.m. I know because I look. I look because Benny never wakes me up. But he's head butting me. Head to head. Like a slow-motion woodpecker, it's that rhythmic. Coming to, and going straight to a communicative consciousness, I say, "OK. Got it." He cheek marks my lips and walks back to sleep between Jill and me.

Our house-call vet isn't back yet, so as early as we can get an appointment, at 2:00 that afternoon, we're in the clinic. We pull up; Benny is in my lap. Even though he couldn't give a shit and is actually wary of what I show him, I present the world blurring past the car, and crack the window so he can smell the ocean. This is, after all, our final destination together. I have him wrapped in a purple chenille blanket that my friend Sorcha gave him back when she first met him. With all of the shit that I've "gypsied" out of our lives along the way, it's this wrap, with loops of fabric pulled loose by the kneading of Benny and his many coconspirators, that will accompany him, the only piece of familiar traveling to this sterile place. Jill will wait in the car, as she does. She has never been able to stand the pain of this loss. It's OK— she has cared for, saved so many; who am I to split hairs? This part of the job has always been uniquely mine and I'm more than fine with it. I take Benny into the side entrance of the clinic and straight into a room. I hate this room. The feel, the energy, the sympathy tinged with after-lunch sleepiness by the staff, the techs. . . . The vet gets rave reviews from my clients, and this still feels wrong. It's setting off every alarm in my psychic arsenal. The bells, the sirens, the barking of the dogs that tell me the fortress is under imminent attack.

And it just gets more wrong—I hate feeling out of control, sure, but not having choices? Being told *this is the way it HAS to be?* Tremors of panic seep through every fight-or-flight muscle in my body. I want out, not because I don't want to live up to my end of the bargain, but because I just want this to be, I don't know, *better.*

It's not going to be better.

The tech feels inexperienced, or at the very least I think I'm making her very nervous. And that makes *me* very nervous. If my energy is dominating this space, then I am forgetting who is in charge here; the universe is in charge. *God, grant me the serenity . . .* She forgets the elementary step of warming up the injectables by rolling the refrigerated bottle in her hands so when she sticks Benny with the "take the edge off" sedation, the freezing liquid poke sends him convulsing, and, of course, hacking. Out comes my glare. The tech is wise and leaves without a word. Folding myself around the top of him like a human tent in the predawn frost, I realize that this will be the last time I ever get to protect him from harm, from pain, from confusion, from anybody who considers him "unbondable." What an amazing universe, I think. Two broken-winged magpies collided and rebuilt each other. This has been his first spin around the incarnational merry-go-round as a cat. I could teach him a thing or two because, as I'll discover, this is my first time around on two legs. We found our way.

I also realize this will be the only chance I have at a proper sendoff to the next life. I want him to know one thing, something he can clutch like a piece of my clothing with him as he wakes up next time; I want him to remember being loved so much that all else will be forgotten. No episodic memory; just an unbroken lifetime of embrace. I lean in tight as I hear the vet enter behind me: "I will tell your story. You hear me? I promise. I keep my promises, right?" The vet is hovering. I already don't like her. I tell him so, but say it's OK—just another shot. You've seen plenty of those.

And I hold my center. He knows me so well, as has every animal who has passed through my hands in this lifetime.

Cat Daddy

This isn't about showing off by lying my way past the cat polygraph; this is aligning with the will of the universe, sur-rendering to it, allowing its water to bathe us both. I'm not, at that moment, sad; I'm overwhelmingly grateful. So many an-imals I've known for such short periods of time. So many I've tried to comfort like this in a dark room, after they'd been abused, discarded, or just ignored by humans. My story with Benny is, in comparison, an embarrassment of riches. And after all, as the song says, love is stronger than death.

The vet and the tech (a different one—the first was rightly scared for her life) do what they have to but my arms are around him the whole time. They are literally moving through the gaps in me like a macabre game of Twister. A quicksandy voice is asking me to move. I have *way* too much experience doing this. Again, I've become expert at communicating with looks. *I'm giving you plenty of room. Work around me.*

I need to protect him from the fluorescent harshness of the unknown. I am full of guilt about not letting this happen at home, so I create a home so big with my body that he will see and feel it, like I'm holding up an IMAX panorama on my shirt.

"I keep my promises, right?"

His breathing slows. I have to give him permission. Like your children shoot you one nervous glance as they put their feet on the school bus and with a slow blink you tell them that the ride will be a good one. The purple blanket will keep you safe. On cue, mercy descends; with my lips on his head, he takes a clear, unsnarfled, untumored, unwheezy breath.

He takes another.

"I keep my promises," I whisper. "I told you when we moved here that the ocean would cure you."

And then, with a gentle spasm, the school bus drives off, taking my brave Benny to the next beautiful stop. Leaving me holding a reminder that bodies are just experiments. Glass to hold the mercury.

Momentary consolation for those watching the bus, waving the gravel dust from their hair.

I'm not breathing.

"You can stay here as long as you want, and then we'll blah blah blah blah. . . ."

His voice fades into the background.

Not breathing.

Please leave, please leave, please.

Not breathing.

The door clicks.

Breathe.

In my lap, wrapped in chenille, we took him to the pet cemetery to have them perform a private cremation. I was very specific to the very understanding woman working the desk; please burn half of the blanket with him and keep the rest for his burial. If one thing was planned to the letter it was this. When I was in Colorado, the five cats I buried were all in the same place, up along Boulder Creek, before the tunnel carved out of Sugarloaf Mountain. It brought me bits of comfort every time I would drive past and blow five kisses. I couldn't do that for Benny; I didn't know my new surroundings well enough to pick the right place. California law requires cremation of dead pets, given the chances of some critter digging them up as quick as they're buried. But I didn't like cremation, so I had to create a picture that would comfort me, that I could live with.

We dug a hole in the backyard and bought a tangerine tree, to remind me of the lush promises I had made Benny when leaving the mountains. I placed the piece of blanket in the hole and then emptied the ashes on top. Finally the dirt and the tree. Long after we left this crumbling old beach home, tangerine gifts would be here for anyone who wanted them. The backyard also had a lemon tree, and we planted plum trees that day as well.

My ritual wasn't complete; there is a small matter of the "ridding." Just like I gypsy my belongings whenever moving on, it was important to me to remove Benny's stuff. This is something I've always done to assist my grieving process. I also do this to help the animals left in the home begin to move through their own reshuffling of the societal deck. Benny's scent, and the markers that uniquely symbolize his presence, needed to go. That meant his food dish, the last vestiges of his dry food, and the airtight container that held it, the brown bed, each and every prescription bottle, syringe, and pill crusher. His collar was all that was left, and that was wrapped in a swath of purple chenille under a new tangerine tree. Love is stronger than death; I need no souvenirs.

As anyone knows who has lost an animal companion, the immediacy of the loss blows through you as if you were an abandoned farmhouse. I began to summon pictures: Benny entering a room like the newly reincarnated bus driver, or even smacking Jen upside the head for daring to bring tension into his territory. The image of the spot on his nose takes me back to the first time I opened that cardboard box on the way to have him X-rayed. Every internal sketch contains a loose thread that unravels me. That first couple of days seesaw from the workaday to the devastated in seconds.

We all say to one another, "It never gets easier." Well, of course not; I would hope not, anyway. If it did, it would mean that it wasn't the companion that died, but something inside us along the way.

Cat Daddy

No, it doesn't get easier, but grief does become predict-able. Having gone through the incredible depths and sud-denness, and, yes, the guilt that you feel for caring more about the passing of a four-legged than some two-leggeds—at the very least you don't stop midbreakdown to wonder "What's *wrong* with me??" You just experience the inconsol-able present, and move on to the next moment. Walking to school growing up, I would go up 82nd from Broadway to the park. When I hung a left at Central Park West, especially in the fall and winter, an incredible blast of wind would hit me as I cleared the last building on the corner. It ran through you like a car and took your breath completely away. Now, nobody likes having their breath taken away—but once you realize that it *will happen*, and with clockwork regularity, you give into it, prepare for it, and remember that breath-ing returns to your body, regardless of whether you pan-icked about it or not.

At the end of the first day in more than thirteen years without Benny, I had Velouria in my lap and could, for this first moment in I don't even know how long, sit. I could hear the sea lions barking in the distance, coming in and out of audio focus like a tornado siren. The way in which I give touches to the top of Velouria's head is as subconsciously appreciative as the way in which she receives them. If I weren't so exhausted, I might actually feel guilty. The chair consumes me and I am peaceful. Sad. But peaceful. I begin to think about the incredible walk Benny and I took together. Mostly I begin to think about the nature of love and my sudden awareness of my ability to experience all of it.

When I began this journey, I was determinedly in the "off" position. As a matter of fact, I didn't even recognize that a journey needed to be taken. I had a job to do; I had to get my songs out to the world. I had a plan. But, as the Yiddish proverb says, "We plan, God laughs." All along, I gathered passion-shaped puzzle pieces, putting them in my pocket until the universe decided I could handle the real picture. My fascination with the ghost in the machine was the reason I had to write verse and chorus, then unhinge my jaw like a snake to sing them; the reason I had to write these songs sitting on New York sidewalks, watching the gait and tics of the strange bodies in extreme motion; the reason I needed to speak or sing to audiences, feeling the divine between all of us; and, of course, the reason, when the universe decided I was ready, that animals electrified my core, suddenly bathing the road behind and ahead with a halogen-tinged hallelujah.

In those days of flailing for connection with the divine without knowing or acknowledging such things, I was tattooed, pierced, punched, kicked, kissed, licked, and stroked in increasingly desperate ways, until finally I fell backward into the waiting arms of a shelter full of homeless animals and they began peeling away the bulky sweaters I had covered myself in. It had taken years—but it started on that first day of work at HSBV.

And I realize, as I break down for the umpteenth time today, cradling Velouria in my arms and sobbing slowly so as not to lose her, that after sixteen years, this, *this* is the moment when I finally take the universe off hold. The original impact in the water from my first days at the shelter has been rippling through me all this time, and now that I have removed all the layers of shrinkwrap I've spent decades covering myself in, the ripples have finally reached the surface. All of the songs that make up my history suddenly make sense—not in an adolescent teen vampire kind of way but in a way that shows that we are all connected by the permanence of love and loss, the original inhabitants of the soul.

Epilogue

On my first day at HSBV I befriended a Pit Bull named Smiley. We became fast and hard friends. Later that week I had my first experience with euthanasia, cradling, reassuring, and seeing off a Pit Bull who easily could have been Smiley save for the human abuse he had suffered that made him terrified of the shelter. Those two dogs proved to be the genesis, the two opposite sides of the flag I raised and, over the years, unfurled. As my ability to love two dogs expanded, some days against every grain of my will, to rooms of cats, blowing forty-five kisses in the middle of the night, and then wider still, slowly, to every cat and dog alive, and beyond, my ability to love became continentally huge. Today, right now, as I sit here writing, still reeling in the wake of a forced awakening, it actually is all coming to me.

Hopefully, you're reading this because you've made a

connection with an animal before. You've had *your* Benny. Or maybe you haven't yet, but you will. Or you want to. My message, the message from all of us in the animal welfare community, is simple: Take a picture of *your* Benny, put it in an imaginary locket. Then, with the love you feel for *your* Benny, hold it in your hands so tightly that you become an alchemist; the love you feel for one becomes the love you feel for all. It is all one. Let the love you feel for *your* Benny expand until it is love for *all* Bennys.

The world is full of cats who need homes, wonderful, exhilarating, maddening cats. Let them into your life. If you don't neuter or spay your animal companion, and they have a litter of twelve kittens, say, you may have shown your children the miracle of birth, and it may be one of the cutest things ever watching those kittens grow, explore, and learn to love the world around them. But know that, on the other end of that string, twelve cats in your neighborhood shelter die the next day. The math is simple and irrefutable.

We can achieve a world where no animals have to die needlessly; today, I truly believe this, to the core of my being. The responsibility we have is toward the alchemy that has nothing to do with our heads. I spent SO many years looking for the unifying theories of behavior—what makes cats tick? Why do *cats* do this? Why do *cats* do that? It's simply just a waste of our collective breath. It saddens me so much when I think of the flawed understanding that protected me from loving that boy too much. Theorizing, explaining away, predicting behavior, empirical data—these are the psuedoscientific mechanisms that kept *him* at a distance, and kept the lessons at bay until now, some time after the dust from his passing has settled. Learn the story of your cat, but not like I learned the story of Benny; learn the lessons in *animal time*, assimilating ecstatic love and debilitating pain in the present moment. If you want to love them, learn to love like they do—firmly in the now.

Take the love you feel for one and love all. The process, I'm here to say, is terrifying. Loving the world is not like the trust fall exercise you did in EST, summer camp, or your last corporate retreat; loving the world is far bigger than that, far riskier, and far more impossible. And if you're like me, you continually ask the universe to come closer, like a stranger you're trying to pick up at a bar. When you kiss the universe passionately and she says she loves you, however, you run as fast and as far as you can, as if she were the cartoon skunk.

I feel blessed on this day. Ultimately, learning Benny's story expanded my ability to diagnose the needs of other cats, yes, but more than that it also expanded my ability to love, expanded it to a degree I simply didn't think was possible, because "think" can't understand love. In this new world order, there are no whiteboards. There is only exploring empathy and acting with sympathy.

In recovery, we talk about *acting as if*. If you don't feel human, if you're walking around white knuckling, if you can't surrender, *act as if* you do, *act as if* you're not, *act as if* you can. Suit up and show up. Someday you will feel comfortable in the beautiful clothes you picked out. I'm writing a letter to you, the cat-loving world, in the suit I picked out for myself. I don't have letters after my name. I'm not a scientist. I'm not a vet. And they are not me, either. I'm a storyteller, and I have spent most of my life learning how to inhabit the lives of others and how to tell those stories with accuracy and with to-my-bones truth.

I feel the everyday lives of every cat I've ever met. Benny was just the first to thumb his nose completely at my efforts, as if to spit at me, incensed at my efforts to pigeonhole him. But I will always be grateful to the universe for putting that cardboard carrier on my path, because the truths he wrote on me can never be erased.

Acknowledgments

First, to my compadres in animal sheltering. In my first days, thirsty for knowledge and challenge, Sunny, Lisa, Bridgette, Laura, Brad, Lizann, Teresa, Sarah, Lesli, Lauren, Jason, and Nana—you provided the foundation of support, laughter, creative argument, education, and challenge to get me through to the next day. I can pay it forward thanks to what you all gifted me. Also to Jan and Dori—sometimes, against your better judgment, you gave me the room to spread my wings, helping to transform a short-term job into a mission and a career. Finally, to the cat and mobile volunteers—Leslie, Peggy, Larry, and so many more—every day with you was a gift in compassion and education.

To my family, who, as beleaguered as I'm sure they were at my consistently off-kilter choice of career path (so much for having something to fall back on!), never wavered in their support of and pride in me as an individual. Thank you for loving me, even when I was unlovable, destructive, and numb.

To Jill, for reminding me of my purpose, even when the big picture threatened to sweep me away. You kept my head attached to my body, my body to my feet, and my feet to the ground. No matter what and no matter when, you will be my family.

To Joy, my literary champion. Your belief in my words is why Benny will live on.

To Joel, for providing the beautiful skeleton and supporting me selflessly and confidently as I learned to build skin.

To the wonderful shepherds of Tarcher/Penguin, Sara Carder and Brianna Yamashita, for allowing me to go away and write, and supporting to the nth degree what I came back with. And thank you, Saryta Rodriguez, for being the messenger when I missed every deadline in sight.

To Ken, thank you for keeping me alive when that was the absolute last thing I thought I wanted.

To Jean, you told me so!

To Todd and Kate, for staying in the crazy and believing in the sound as long as you did.

To the caring tenders of this garden—Siena Lee-Tajiri, Toast Tajiri, Heather Curtis, Adam Greener, J. D. Roth, Brian Rochlin, Susan Von Seggern, David Wollock, Rob Cohen, Mike and Tami Bloom, Lindsay Wineberg, Mark De-

Acknowledgments

genkolb, and Melinda Toporoff. Thank you for taking the chance and giving this work room to be created.

To the ones who talked me through the jungle—Diane Israel, Stephanie Rasband, Amy Kisch, Craig Chesler, Diana Dawson, Bobby Colomby, Kate Benjamin, Peter Wolf, Minoo Rahbar, Adam Kaloustian, Sarah Pettit, and Steve Maresca. The bravery it takes to write does not come alone.

To every dopeless hope fiend the world over. The promises are real.

Love, Light & Cat Mojo—
Jackson Galaxy

If you enjoyed this book, visit

www.tarcherbooks.com

and sign up for Tarcher's e-newsletter to receive special offers, giveaway promotions, and information on hot upcoming releases.

TARCHER
PENGUIN

Great Lives Begin with Great Ideas

If you would like to place a bulk order of this book, call 1-800-847-5515.